TECHNOLOGICAL ASPECTS OF VIRTUAL ORGANIZATIONS

TECHNOLOGICAL ASPECTS OF VIRTUAL ORGANIZATIONS

Enabling the Intelligent Enterprise

By

ALEA M. FAIRCHILD, Ph.D.
Vesalius College / Vrije Universiteit Brussel, Belgium and Greiner International, Inc.

Contribution by Bruno de Vuyst, Advocaat (Chapter 4, section 3)

Kluwer Academic Publishers
Boston/Dordrecht/London

Library of Congress Cataloging-in-Publication Data is available.

ISBN 1-4020-1732-4

Published by Kluwer Academic Publishers
PO Box 17, 3300 AA Dordrecht, The Netherlands

Sold and distributed in North, Central and South America
by Kluwer Academic Publishers,
101 Philip Drive, Norwell, MA 02061, U.S.A.

In all other countries, sold and distributed
by Kluwer Academic Publishers, Distribution Centre,
PO Box 322, 3300 AH Dordrecht, The Netherlands

Printed on acid-free paper

Printed in Great Britain by MPG Books Limited, Bodmin, Cornwall.

This book is dedicated to my husband Bruno and son Michael, for their strong support of my endeavours

Contents

INTRODUCTION

This textbook was inspired by an undergraduate elective course given on virtual organizations and technology. The instructor could not find a suitable text that covered both the organizational and technological aspects including examples based on today's industry. Other books were either too strategic or too technical for an audience of undergraduate business and technology students who were to use the book. But why was that the case?

For the same reason that business and IT people in industry tended not to speak the same "language": indeed, the integration of technology into business strategy has been a recent occurrence, and traditional strategy issues have been decided too high in the organizational structure while technology was too detailed in tactical implementation. With the Internet and the advent of e-commerce, m-commerce, and c-commerce (and the other letters of the alphabet soon to follow), business and technology finally started to become closer, and the interest in technology as an enabler for strategic business decision-making evolved into a mainstream concept.

How are we defining a virtual organization? Most definitions of the concept of virtual organizations start with stating that it is "a network between organisations or individuals ...". The Oxford Concise Dictionary defines 'virtual' as: *"that is such for practical purposes, though not in name or according to a strict definition."* An organization may be thought of as a number of individuals systematically united for some end or work. Perhaps in this case, we can view a virtual organization as a number of individuals united with a practical purpose, or a practical structure for the 21st century.

The evolution of virtual organizations, based on economic principle and technological advance, has either focused on process or on structure within the organization. Table 1 (from Saabeel *et al.*, 2002) shows how the literature has reflected these two views.

Table 1. Authors and their main focus on virtual organizations

Perspective	Author	Terminology
Structure	Bryne (1993)	Network
	Aken *et al.* (1998)	Network
	Strader *et al.* (1998)	Network
	Wilderman (1998)	Alliance
	Grenier and Metes (1995)	Alliance
	Wüthrich and Phillips (1998)	Form of co-operation
	Mertens *et al.* (1988)	Form of co-operation
	Goldman *et al.* (1995)	Combination of core competencies
	Davidow and Malone (1993)	Combination of activities
Process	Hale and Whitlaw (1997)	Continuous or institutionalized change
	Venkatraman and Henderson (1996)	Strategic approach
	Mowshowitz (1997)	Management approach
	Katzy (1998)	Action or ability

If so many have segmented virtual organization in the literature, why are technological aspects important for us? It must be because technology is an enabling infrastructure to connect the structure of an organization to its processes.

The constituting elements of a virtual organization, which is a set of independent organizations and their mutual relationships, should possess characteristics that enable them to function as a single organization to reach a common goal. For the network as a whole this implies that requirements posed by competitive and dynamic environment have to be fulfilled by leveraging the benefits of being a network of organizations, which includes the technical benefit of the network as well – a point rarely discussed in the previous literature.

This textbook is designed for both undergraduate business and technology (CS) programs, as well as graduate management programs.

Chapter 1

INDIVIDUALS AND TECHNOLOGY INTERFACES

Introduction

The role of the individual in virtual organizations is critical, as the base unit of analysis of an organization is the individual and the contribution of the individual to the collective organizational knowledge. To integrate both people and technology and to accommodate the intellectual possibilities of cyberspace and cyber valley companies, a broad perspective is necessary. The concept of interfaces opens up such a perspective. In our understanding, interfaces have a number of distinct features.

Learning Objectives of the Chapter

When you have completed this chapter, you should be able to:

- Examine how human beings interface with others via the Internet;
- Recognize the advantages and disadvantages of hypertext;
- Identify uses of multimedia applications in the virtual organization.

1.1 Use of Technology by Individuals, in the Context of Virtual Organizations

1.1.1 Interfaces: Synthesis of People and Technology

Interfaces are temporary networks of people and/or computers, integrating human beings as well as intelligent agents and databases. They only exist by means of inter-subjective construction and maintenance. Interfaces are, in other words, socio-technological actor-networks (Callon 1986: 28–34).

But why does an actor act and why are networks dynamic? The Actor-Network Theory has paid little attention to those questions. The acting actor and the dynamic network are presupposed as a given; they develop simply "deliberately or otherwise" (Law and Callon, 1992, p.21). However, while actors in networks thrive towards convergence and stability, one of the central aims of the theory is to account for dynamics, change and innovation (Law and Callon, 1992). Actor-networks are always potentially dynamic; they are subject to evolution on all scales and in all places.

In contrast to closed system concepts (e.g. organizations), interfaces have open structures, thereby enabling constant bifurcation that can lead to new solutions. Hence, interfaces are very flexible in their adaptation to new realities.

The construction of interfaces does not follow a simple human or technological logic. Instead, in interfaces computer and human logic is intertwined: interfaces expand human thinking electronically by "copying" the functional principles of the human brain, allowing human-based computer thinking. Interfaces also provide a digital coding and decoding of cyberspace and (virtual) realities, providing for computer-based human thinking.

Interfaces evolve through a continuous process of participation and feedback. Bi-directional feedback loops between interface and participant secure a two-fold responsibility for both individual and interface activity, which creates a trustful environment in which individuals are willing to participate. With their capacity of simulation, evolution in interfaces can be reversible, in contrast to the irreversible evolution of physical worlds. With the advance of interface technologies (nanotechnology, quantum computers, biotechnology) this permits new human life configurations and the formation of a global brain with a possible meta-consciousness.

With such an interface perspective, it is possible to address both human as well as technical questions of collective intelligence. Such a perspective will also change some of the paradigmatic principles guiding our epistemological and managerial understanding.

Endo (Greek 'from inside') means that we are inside an interface – a constructed borderline of our knowledge. Interfaces as a lens for construction of reality allow us to make an *endo-/exo-* cut between the knowledge of a network or a participant and the outside world. *Exo* (Greek 'outside') means that we are outside of this interface.

We can therefore state that any virtual world is *endo* to a physical world, but not every *endo*-world has to be virtual. With this *endo/exo* distinction one can (analytically) cut through the fluidity of interfaces.

What most newcomers in the Internet do not understand is that the main topic in the Internet is not to sell an *exo*-product or an *exo*-service, but to connect people in order to communicate. They mistakenly believe that the Internet is constructed as digital copy of the physical *exo*-world. Yet, it is a living electronic *endo*-world with its own rationale. It has no owner (if at all, the Global Brain is the 'owner'). And it is still largely a non-regulated world. The most important rule in the Internet is to minimize the number of rules to provide enough space for different interfaces to connect. The main currency is attention. Hence, a constant effort has to be put in to maintain it and attract participation. And the Internet does not follow the same causal logic as some of the *exo*-worlds do, which leads to non-linear dynamics and chaotic patterns of events. Yet, one thing should be kept in mind:

Endo-worlds and exo-worlds are not two worlds clearly distinguishable; they are more like a seamless meta-interface itself.

1.1.2 Study of HCI

Human–computer interaction (HCI) is a discipline concerned with the design, evaluation and implementation of interactive computing systems for human use and with the study of major phenomena surrounding them (Hewett *et al.*, 1992).

From a computer science perspective, the focus is on interaction and specifically on interaction between one or more humans and one or more computational machines. The classical situation that comes to mind is a person using an interactive graphics program on a workstation. But it is clear that varying what is meant by interaction, human, and machine leads to a rich space of possible topics.

For example, Fitts' Law is a robust model of human psychomotor behavior developed in 1954. Commonly in HCI, Fitts' Law is used to evaluate input devices. The model is based on time and distance. It enables the prediction of human movement and human motion based on rapid, aimed movement, not drawing or writing. Fitts' Law states: "*The time to acquire a target is a function of the distance to and size of the target*". What this means is that the bigger an item is, the easier it is to click, and the easiest item to locate on the screen is one that is closest to the mouse pointer and largest in size. Other than size and proximity, position on the screen is also an important factor in 'ease of click.' Fitts went into a great deal of depth about his law. He developed formulas to measure the impact of different velocities, distances, and target sizes on a user's 'ease of click.'

HCI is important in virtual organizations in that it is a specialty concern within several disciplines, each with different emphases: computer science (application design and engineering of human interfaces), psychology (the application of theories of cognitive processes and the empirical analysis of user behavior), sociology and anthropology (interactions between technology, work, and organization), and industrial design (interactive products). HCI is concerned with the joint performance of tasks by humans and machines; the structure of communication between human and machine; human capabilities to use machines (including the learnability of interfaces); algorithms and programming of the interface itself; engineering concerns that arise in designing and building interfaces; the process of specification, design, and implementation of interfaces; and design trade-offs. HCI therefore has science, engineering, and design aspects (Hewett *et al.*, 1992).

Human factors, as a discipline, derives from the problems of designing equipment operable by humans during World War II (Sanders & McCormick, 1987). Many problems faced by those working on human factors had strong sensory-motor features (e.g., the design of flight displays and controls). The problem of the human operation of computers was a natural extension of classical human factors concerns, except that the new problems had substantial cognitive, communication, and interaction aspects not previously developed in human factors, forcing a growth of human factors in these directions. Ergonomics is similar to human factors, but it arose from studies of work. As with human factors, the concerns of ergonomics tended to be at the sensory-motor level, but with an additional physiological flavor and an emphasis on stress. Human interaction with computers was also a natural topic for ergonomics, but again, a cognitive extension to the field was necessary resulting in the current "cognitive ergonomics" and "cognitive engineering." (Hewett *et al.*, 1992).

Interfaces to allow groups of people to coordinate are becoming more common (e.g., for meetings, for engineering projects, for authoring joint documents). These can have major impacts on the nature of organizations and on the division of labor. Models of the group design process are becoming embedded in systems and will cause increased rationalization of design.

In an extensive examination of general HCI principles and guidelines, Hardman and Sharratt (1989) have highlighted those principles relevant to hypertext systems, and defined their usage within the hypertext domain. Interaction is seen as using an application's dynamic functionality through operating on presentation elements. Several of these principles are of particular importance within a program understanding hypertext system.

1.2 Hypertext

Hypertext consists of linked segments of text or other information. Of course, ordinary text is linked in as much as one paragraph follows another in sequence (or one page follows another); it is usual to reserve the term 'hypertext' for the instance in which there might be several links emanating from a particular source; hence the linking is non-sequential because the notion of next item is not unique (for there might be several 'next' items). If the focus of the system is to facilitate learning primarily through non-textual modes of information transfer (i.e., graphics, animation, video, sound), then the term multimedia (or hypermedia) applies (Nielsen, 1990).

Hypertext is not easy to implement through traditional media. Indeed, how can a page in a book have two or more next pages? Only by such artifices as breaking the connection between page numbers do we attain the notion of 'next page'; we assume that the next page to page 35 is page 36 but if page 35 were to have on it that the reader should continue with page 70 (if they liked excitement) or page 40 (if they did not) then page 35.

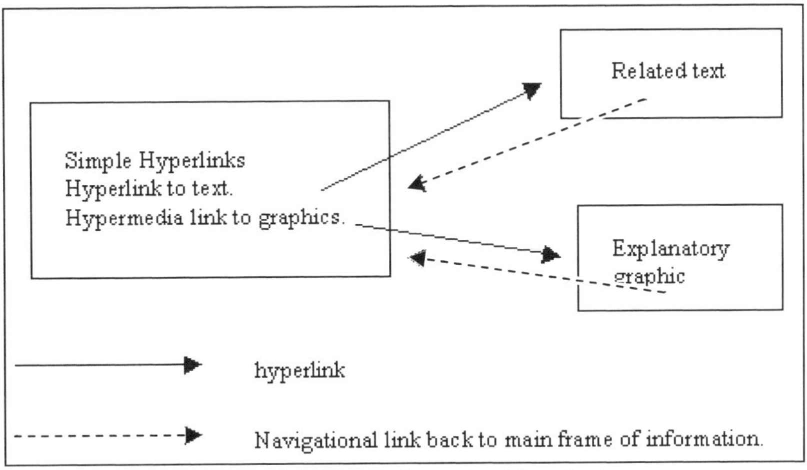

Figure 1.1. Hyperlink structural flowchart

Figure 1.1 (above) shows a very simple hyperlink structure where links are made from the main page or frame of information to another text frame and to a graphic item that may be a video clip, animated image or photographic image. A navigational link is provided to get back to the main frame of information. Full hypermedia systems have links that are much more complex; this is a simple diagram to demonstrate a hyperlink structure.

Hypertext and hypermedia are predominantly electronic possibilities as they are new document forms made possible by technology.

According to Roy Rada (1991) the term hypertext is related in purpose to the idea of 'hyperbolic space' used by the 19th century mathematician F. Klein (1849–1929). In his writings Klein used *hyperspace* as the description of a geometry with multiple dimensions. Hypertext, therefore, is supposed to be a form of multi-dimensional text that can potentially model the "hyperspace" of concepts that would be implicit in almost every text. Rada explains that one should view the purpose of hypertext as an extension of text; the text itself has its own internal structure or dimensions, whereas hypertext illuminates this structure and adds further dimensions. The latter includes microtext, the relations among components of one document; macrotext, relations among several documents; and grouptext, in which individuals directly communicate or collaborate on a project. Furthermore, the control of these dimensions would be invested in either the designer or the user depending upon the desired level of user autonomy.

A more concrete realization of the purpose of hypertext can be elicited from the significant events of its rather interesting history. Let us examine a synopsis of these events.

1.2.1 Aspects of the History of Hypertext (modified text from Nielson, 1990)

Information by association – 1945. Vannevar Bush, the famous scientist and advisor to President Roosevelt, was considered the 'grandfather' of hypertext because he proposed the first ideas for a working system. He called it Memex, "a sort of mechanized private file and library" on microfilm in which an individual stores books, writings, etc. which could be accessed quickly and flexibly. Bush was primarily concerned about the explosion of scientific information beyond the point where anyone would be able to follow developments in a discipline.

Augment/NLS – 1962–76. Doug Englebart started work in 1962 on his ambitious Augment project at Stanford Research Institute (SRI), to develop computer tools for improving human productivity and capabilities. One part of the project was NLS (oN-Line System) which had several hypertext features. During the project, researchers stored all their papers, reports, etc. in a shared journal that grew to over 100,000 items. The project actually invented or inspired much of modern interactive computing.

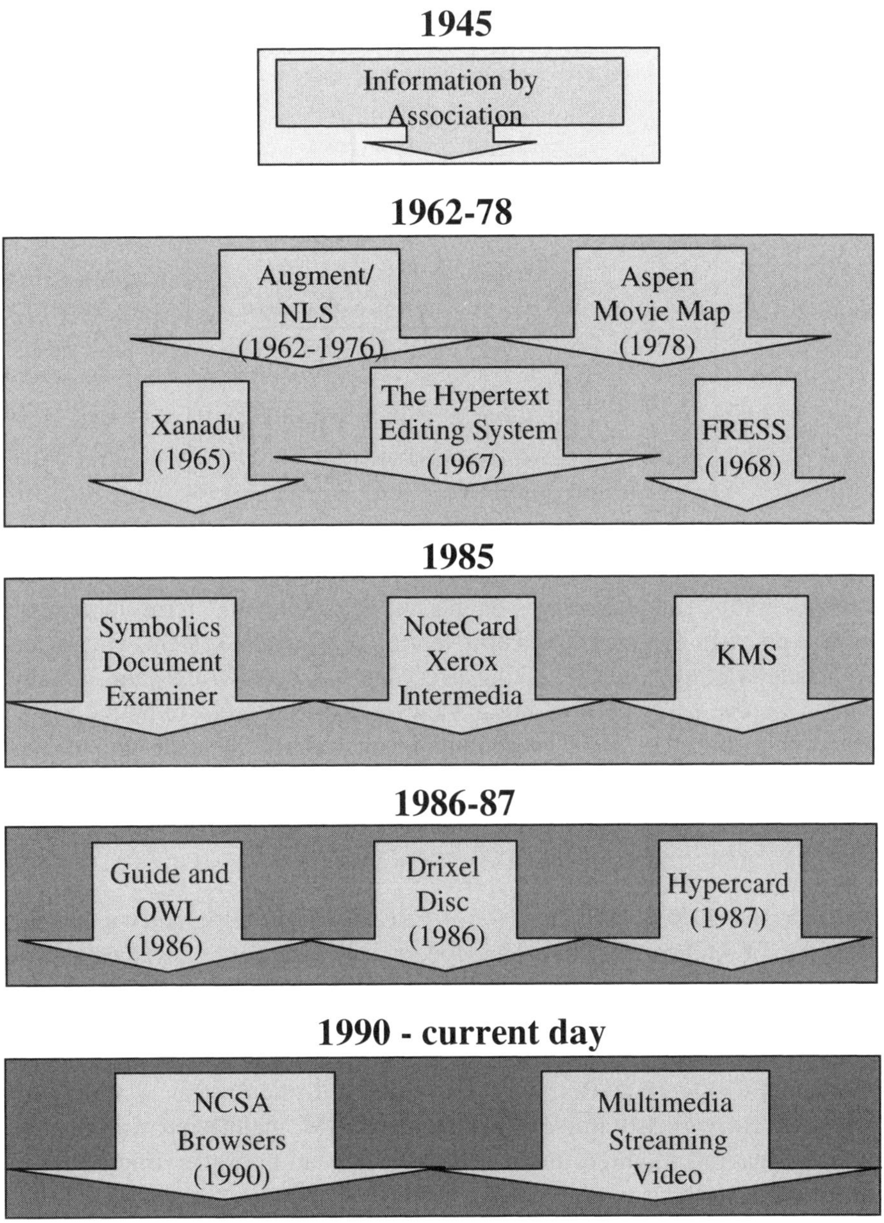

Figure 1.2. Timeline of Hypertext (source: Nielson, 1990)

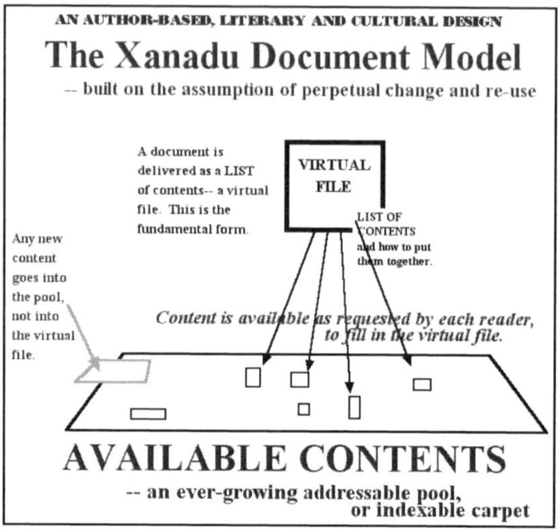

Figure 1.3. The Xanadu Model, source: xanadu.com

Xanadu – 1965. Ted Nelson was the person who coined the term 'hypertext' and was an early hypertext pioneer inventing the Xanadu system. The vision of Xanadu was to store everything everyone has ever written and thereby achieve a universal hypertext. In his view, everything needs to be on-line in a literary medium because everything is interrelated. The design idea is based on a combination of local databases for information used the most, and 'back end' repositories for more esoteric information to be linked into the network as needed.

The Hypertext Editing System – 1967; FRESS – 1968. Originally under the leadership of Andres van Dam, The Hypertext Editing System was created at Brown University. It was the world's first completely functional hypertext system, funded by an IBM research contract, and later sold to the Houston Manned Spacecraft Center where it produced documents for the Apollo missions. FRESS (File Retrieval and Editing System) was a follow-up system at Brown also implemented on an IBM mainframe. Linking or jumping locations required 'indirect' user specification of the jumps through a text-based interface.

Aspen Movie Map – 1978. Developed by Andrew Lippman and a team at MIT, this was probably the first true hypermedia system. It presented a simulated travel experience to the city of Aspen, Colorado, utilizing a set of videodiscs which contained a complete photographic record of the city's streets. Hypermedia aspects are based on accessing the pictures as linked sets of information, not like a traditional database. As a follow-up, the MIT group built a Movie Manual for car and bike repairs; the user would point to parts of a picture (e.g., a car) to get information via images, video, and text.

Symbolics Document Examiner – 1985. The Document Examiner was the first hypertext system to be successful as a product for real-world use. 'Real' users of Symbolics equipment (engineers using advanced artificial intelligence workstations) found the approach to be very effective, although these were sophisticated users accustomed to high technology solutions. The Document Examiner was a hypertext interface to online documentation; an 8,000 page manual was represented by 10,000 nodes of hypertext with 23,000 links requiring a total storage space of ten megabytes. The basic principle was to have a node for anything users might want.

KMS, commercial successor of ZOG. KMS stands for Knowledge Management System, whereas ZOG was a nickname for the original research system developed at Carnegie Mellon University in the 1970s. It runs on Sun and Apollo workstations and has been used for many applications. KMS is based on a simple data structure: one type of node called a frame; the screen could be split into no more than two frames at a time (no resizing or moving windows) with hypertext navigation being used to change the content of the display. It does not provide an overview diagram, but relies on rapid navigation in a hierarchical structure of nodes. It includes a 'home' frame accessible from any location and backtracking by clicking empty space.

Other systems – 1985. Several hypertext systems arrived in the mid-1980s, including NoteCards from Xerox and Intermedia from Brown University. A ZOG frame-based system from Carnegie Mellon was used on the USS Carl Vinson. Of particular interest is Intermedia which provides a highly integrated environment. Intermedia runs under Unix, with scrolling windows, and was designed for educational use at the college level. The model assumes multiple users will access the same hypertext documents and make their own notes and new links. Bi-directional links connect scrolled-to anchors rather than nodes, which encourages authors to construct longer documents because they can easily link to specific points.

Guide and OWL – 1986. The company named OWL (Office Workstations Limited) introduced Guide as a commercial product, the first widely available hypertext to run on desktop computers. For years it was the only available system which could run on both Macs and PCs. Guide was started as a research project by Peter Brown at the University of Kent. Guide is like

NoteCards in being based on scrolling text rather than fixed frames, with the difference that Guide links can scroll-jump to new locations in a file without switching to another card. Anchors are in text strings; the original Guide has three separate types of buttons with associated hypertext linking; replacements (for expansion), pop-ups (for annotations), and reference (for in-file jumps); a later version includes commands (for other media). For all types of links, readers and authors have the same level of access and control.

Drexel Disk, then switching into HyperCard. Drexel University in Pennsylvania was one of the universities that required all students to have a Mac computer; faculty would develop software and be certain that students could run it. The Drexel Disk contained detailed information about the university in a hypertext format. For example, jumps to a campus map were availed for every mention in the text of buildings, and the map included links from buildings to descriptions of departments and facilities. Produced through the years by the Office of Information Resources and Technology (IRT), the first "Drexel Disk" was issued in Fall 1984 as an 800k floppy disk, and went through four versions in that format. It was replaced by an interactive HyperCard stack (Bill Atkinson's HyperCard from Apple) and then, after the advent of CD technology, by the HTML-based "Drexel CD" which is now a prime source of site-licensed software and useful information about Drexel and MCP Hahnemann Universities.

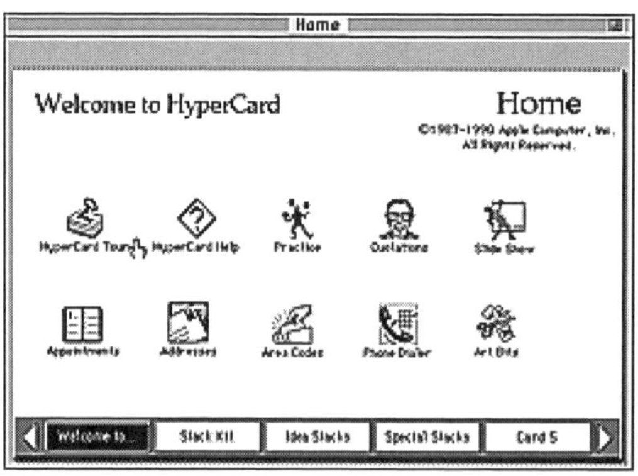

Figure 1.4. HyperCard example

HyperCard – 1987. When Apple introduced HyperCard, it extended awareness of hypertext capabilities to high profile commercial applications software with the marketing concept of providing the program bundled with every Mac computer. HyperCard was a real breakthrough in the recognition and acceptance of hypertext as a medium of information structure for projects.

HyperCard is based on a card metaphor; like KMS, the system uses frames but they are restricted to cards small enough to fit on the original Mac screen. Anchors are set up as graphical regions on the cards. The main advantage of the HyperCard system is the implementation of jumps as Hypertalk programming language statements; that is, any executable code can be a destination. Author access includes much more control than user access.

What is the form of Hypertext? Hypertext, as defined by Ted Nelson in the 1960s, represents the idea of packaging and organizing information in nonlinear structures so that the content can be explored via self-determined linkages (Paine and McAra, 1993). The hypertext environment supports the development of interactive systems which permit learners to deepen or enhance their knowledge by establishing new associations and pathways of understanding (by linking together discrete segments of information).

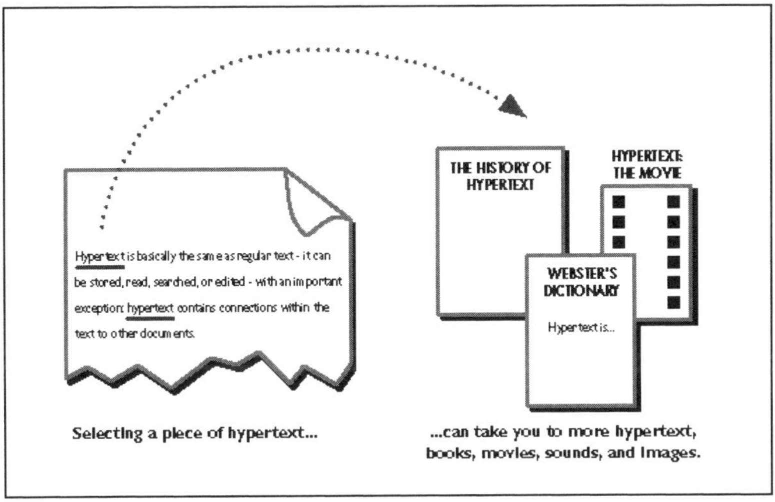

Figure 1.5. Hypertext linking example

As various hypertext systems have been applied to multiple learning and instructional domains, some interesting dimensions of information and knowledge structures have emerged as conceptual variables for the hypertext-systems design process. To understand the scope of the hypertext learning environment, and its relationship to networks of information, consider the following table which describes three important variables by dichotomy .

1.2.2 Conceptual variables for hypertext development (modified from Romiszowski and Abrahamson, 1992)

Associational	vs. Pragmatic
Non-sequential multi-dimensional storage of information is characteristic of the human mind. Association and linking are qualities of creative thinking, and thus it is useful to structure external knowledge bases in a similar way.	*It is impossible to predict the information needs of the individual reader, so it is more effective and economical to structure a knowledge base which can serve the information needs of any reader, with limited 'user-control'.*

Constructivism	vs. Objectivism
Knowledge structures are individual and unique representations of reality from learning and experience. Any hypertext is an external record of a unique structure imposed arbitrarily on a domain of knowledge by its author(s).	*A domain of knowledge can be analyzed, structured, and presented in form which is optimal for learning and reference. The network of information nodes and links represent the inherent structure of the knowledge domain.*

Creativity	vs. Systematics
The network of information nodes and links begin with the act of creativity or insight of the author(s), but does not end there. Any user should be free to annotate or otherwise add to the hypertext.	*Preparing hypertext is a specialist task to be performed by skilled designers for the benefit of many readers. Additions or changes to this structure should only result from systematic planning.*

As may be understood from above, Nelson's concept of hypertext may be summarized in terms of 'nodes' and 'links'. Both Nelson and Vannevar Bush (1945) before him advocated the general approach of storing textual information as a network of documents linked by meaningful pointers (Romiszowski, 1993). By node here we mean the place, document, or file where some of the text, data, information, or pictures are stored. Conceptually this might be a paragraph, a page, or a 'frame'. Text sequential presentation can be modified. In fact, hypertext is intended to be primarily non-sequential, presenting different options to different readers for them to follow at the time of reading (like 'generalized footnotes'). Clicking on a link becomes a simple mode of transfer similar to launching a utility program on a client computer. Any node-link (forwardtrack, sidetrack, or backtrack) therefore represents an opportunity for the learner to assert some control over the presentation of information; as we will see, actuating the link is the beginning of a user-centered learning experience.

As defined, a link takes place by forming a connection between one node and the next. Technically, the link represents a directed graph in the information structure because it points from one place (anchor node) to another place (destination node). Once the learner has established a pathway via several links then backtracking occurs along the same pathway, but nodes along the way would be encountered in reverse order. Some authors have advocated bi-directional links (and displaying them); meaning that, at the user's discretion, one could proceed in either direction after the placement of anchors at both ends. The system could inform the learner not just what links are available to proceed forward, or as a sidetrack, but also what alternative paths could have led to the learner's present location.

Given opportunities to modify search behaviors, which are afforded by computer-based learning systems, what are the possible ways that a learner might utilize such links?

McAleese (1989) summarizes the results of a study by Canter, Rivers, and Storrs (1985) which allows us to compare and contrast the approaches taken by various learners interacting with a database system. They identify five general search strategies:

Scanning – covering a large section of information with little depth.
Browsing – following a certain path until a particular goal is achieved.
Searching – pursuing an explicit goal whether by strategy or otherwise.
Exploring – discovering the extent of information given for a topic or section.
Wandering – purposeless and unstructured traveling through the available material.

An important point which underlies navigating in hypertext is that the structure of information imposes constraints on possible search patterns and learning behaviors as well. Since the objective of authoring in hypertext is to facilitate a not-necessarily sequential choice of pathways through a large knowledge base, the information structures are to be designed with learner discretion in mind.

In developing hypertext, specialized computer software first evolved as 'authoring systems' which focused on linking graphics and text to multiple knowledge targets. The resulting hypertext documents can include several pop-up menus, boxes, and buttons which have pre-defined, built-in links usually designed to transfer attention to a related knowledge structure and text areas, consisting of scrolling areas of text; or graphical objects (images) which can be imported from other sources. Sometimes, the image represents a special type of link called an "imagemap" so that clicking on different parts of the image activates a link to different locations.

Many systems have an explicit representation of their 'network' structure in the user interface; this is just a metaphor to understand linkages between elements in the hypertext, but from the user's perspective it can be misunderstood. McAleese (1989) explains that taken literally a network implies that no particular node is more central or important than any other node. In the ideal network system, every node would be accessible from every other node at a distance of one link; a computer could store all these links, but from a human standpoint, it is difficult to imagine a physical representation of such complexity. A better analogy for organizing information structures is to think of a fishing net with the knots as nodes; one-link access from a given node is only possible to 3 or 4 other nodes. If we visualize picking up one of the knots (nodes) other nodes cascade downward from this apex forming a hierarchy of layers. This hierarchical organization provides a ready basis for purposeful browsing or searching.

McAleese suggests that hypertext, in addition to allowing the "freedom to get lost", can exploit hierarchical layering to provide cognitive schemata for the user to attain learning goals. The point of "ideational scaffolding" (Ausubel, 1974) is to present an organizing framework for information to be learned; in the case of hypertext, a small set of link types can elicit an 'educative' expectation for knowledge acquisition. The user begins to acquire the same hierarchical organization for his own thinking and memory. If not planned and implemented in the user interface, the implicit hierarchy of the hypertext system may still support the learner's ideational scaffolding.

A good example of planned scaffolding is the two types of overview diagrams presented in window-based Intermedia, developed at Brown University. One is a "web view" (not related to the Web, WWW), constructed automatically by the system, which provides the learner with an individualized path record showing which, when, and how documents have been reached; the other is a set of overview documents (flow charts of concepts) constructed by the author for each important learning topic. After Intermedia version 4.0, a funding cut and an incompatible update to the Apple operating system forced discontinuation of work on Intermedia. Brown University now uses Storyspace in its place.

Another illustrative example is the format of adventure games, although they make it difficult to navigate instead of easy, and often require clues.

Why use hypertext? The intent is to provide a greater flexibility for learner-centered access to knowledge, which becomes more than browsing or criss-crossing links among documents. Ultimately, the hypertext models are intended to support learner choices in the mental scaffolding of information. The learner in selecting and pursuing an individualized pathway of knowledge acquisition undertakes new dimensions of understanding.

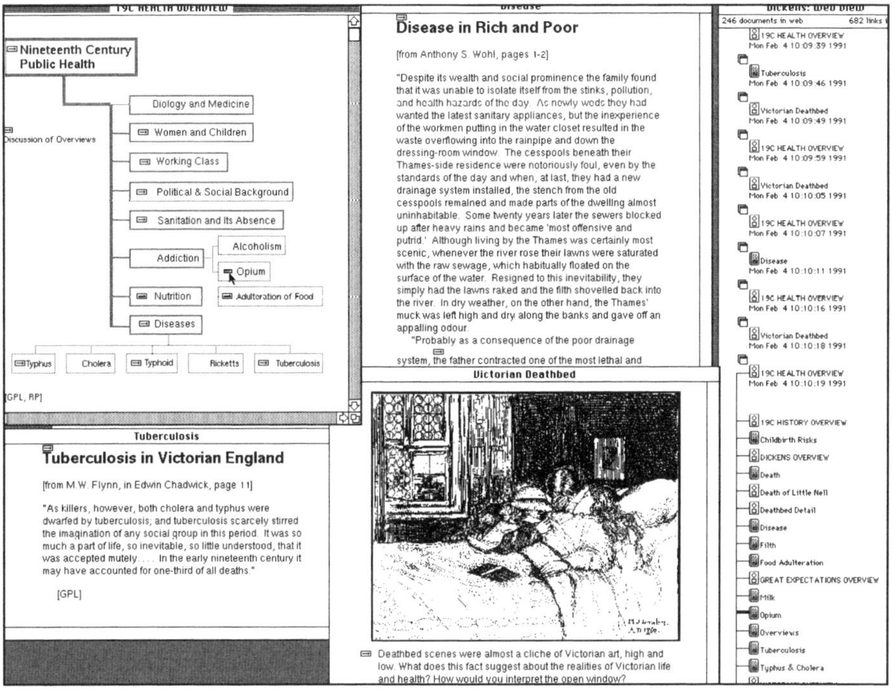

Figure 1.6. Intermedia example

Learning through hypertext can provide continuity to reduce the amount of detail accessed, or, just the opposite, vastly increase the amount of detail available. Esperet (1996) puts it more succinctly, that the defining feature of hypertext is to allow alternative ways of presenting textual information. In this process, users must learn to take advantage of unique presentation formats, including direct links to a myriad of related materials and access to ideas via a hierarchical structure. Ultimately, the result is the opportunity for completely new learning experiences and the acquisition of differentiated text comprehension strategies.

1.2.3 The Architecture of Hypertext Systems

In theory one may distinguish at least three levels in any hypertext system (from Nielsen, 1990):

Database level: storage, shared data, network access.
An important specification for the database is that a designated small chunk of information must be retrievable quickly. When the learner wants to link to

specific information, it will take place in the context of multi-user access to the system. Security considerations, backup, and enforcement of access controls must occur at the database level. To take best advantage of the significant developments in database technology, nodes and links would be data processing objects with meaning only in terms of bits of storage space. Each object would be a discrete unit that only one user can modify at a time.

Hypertext Abstract Machine (HAM) level: nodes and links
This is the middle level of processing where the hypertext system determines the meaning of nodes and links and maintains the relations among them. The HAM would have knowledge of their form and attributes, such as specification of the user who creates the node/link or who can authorize updates or perhaps a version number. Interchange of hypertexts between different systems, especially transfer of information about links, would have to occur at this level; because the database level is too machine dependent and the presentation level is too differentiated for standardization.

Presentation level: user interface
The interface is about how to present information from the HAM, for issues such as command set, how to show links and nodes, and whether or not overview diagrams are included. Decisions at the presentation level are highly dependent on the HAM. For example, the number of link types specified by the HAM would weigh heavily in how the types are displayed; icons could represent several link types but a hypertext with many link types would require naming them with text in the interface. Many other issues are involved at the presentation level, including such basic distinctions as reading versus writing commands, menus, text formats, and other parameters from human factors research.

1.2.4 The Primary User Interface Issues

Most of the existing hypertext systems provide pre-established content in the nodes; that is, the original author controls both the form and substance of the information structures. The locus of control is the first area of concern pertaining to the presentation level of the system. Issues of control include questions such as: Should the system permit only browsing, or allow the learner to do writing into the hypertext? Should the interface design be fixed or adjustable?

Meeting the needs of novices versus experts is highly important even when the range of potential users is somewhat restricted. Learners advance at different rates and relatively soon after a system is placed in use learners will be operating at various levels of sophistication. The novice learners may not be aware of the best order to read the material or what is the most important information; they may be easily sidetracked, distracted, or simply lost. For the novice user it is better to have more system control and less learner control. Of course, the situation is opposite for the expert learner although the degree of learner control which is optimal would vary with the complexity of content. One efficient way to cope with the range of learners is to build an AI (Artificial Intelligence) shell into the system which can set parameters for interface with the information structures according to inputs about learner characteristics.

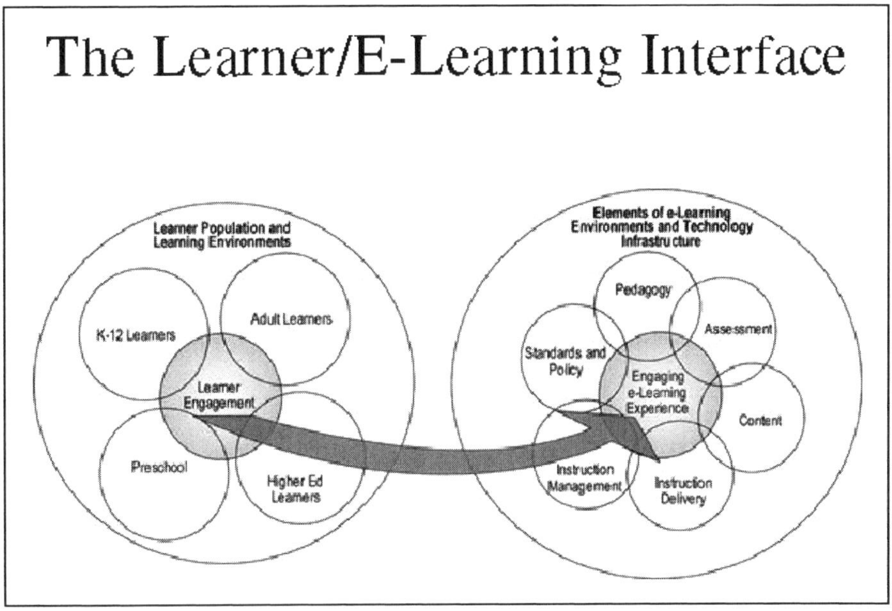

Figure 1.7. E-Learning Interface
(source: Journal of Special Education Technology, Vol. 17.3)

A second area of concern for presentation level is in the appearance, style, and feel of the interaction. A dynamic system, which adjusts as the learner progresses, has many advantages for effectiveness and for motivation. At a minimum, the system must provide a fast response relative to the learner's absorption rate otherwise frustration sets in rather quickly. Every hypertext system displays information visually in some format or style, with particular components such as windows, frames, icons, buttons, fields, etc. The display determines the user-interaction style.

At least four interaction styles have been tried in hypertext systems thus far (Rada, 1991):

- command line: flexible but lacking in meaningfulness, and requires training.
- menu selection: shortens learning, organizes decision-making but slows frequent users;
- natural language: users don't have to learn syntax but may require clarifying dialog;
- direct manipulation: tasks represented visually, best for obtaining an interactive "feel".

Not all variables of component style have comparable significance. Research by Stark (1990) suggests that people's subjective evaluation of window styles may indicate a difference in how cognitively demanding they are; however, window style alone does not systematically effect performance on simple tasks; thus, pop-ups and other forms of simultaneous windowing may not always be superior to "replacement" windows. What pop-ups and simultaneous windowing do allow is more opportunity for learner control of the microtext, which is more relevant for complex tasks and motivation over a course of study.

The screen elements of the browser interface should be an organized layout, which draws attention to the important pieces as well as the links. Also, consistency with any hierarchical view (map) would be a priority. The interface needs to be tailored to the user and the situation. We have already mentioned that requirement of supporting learners with varying ability. Rada (1991) agrees, and notes that different perspectives should be available for potential matching with various learner characteristics, preferences, or objectives. In general, the number of items to choose from at any given time should be limited; and other aspects of design must be evaluated in terms of 'cognitive cost', which is the mental effort required on the part of the learner to utilize any of the available features (Rouet & Levonen, 1996). Rouet and Levonen (1996) cite a 1989 Foss experiment where readers flipped through the nodes of a hypertext without reading them, a result of a disorientation problem. Rouet and Levonen (1996) also point out that hypertext requires a higher cognitive load as the readers attempt to remember their location in the text, make decisions of where to go next, and remember pages previously visited.

Other recommendations for improving the user interface include: invoking a travel metaphor in the sense of a journey through the information; component displays with interesting and meaningful icons attached as guideposts; and provision of extension facilities (customizable or programmable hypertext) which allow sophisticated users to obtain more benefits from the hypertext system.

1.2.5 Some Hypertext-Level Aspects

Whenever we consider the Hypertext Abstract Machine (HAM) level, it is important to remember that the most fundamental units of hypertext are nodes and links. Yet there does not exist a consensus about what really comprises a satisfactory node or how many types of links should be defined. According to Nielsen (1990) the main distinction of concern is between frame-based systems and window-based systems.

The relationship between nodes and links is the heart of the matter. Frames are fixed in size, which then requires that lengthy information be divided among several frames. The advantage of frames is that jumps can take place via any hypertext format in the system. Should anchors be especially prominent? In sparse hypertext, maybe. In rich, not so. By contrast, windows require the learner to scroll through text to find any part of the node, and there is ample capacity for any amount of content in the node. The advantage of windows is that their sizes can be altered according to the size and importance of the information to be conveyed.

Nodes, and the complexity of information contained within them, constitute information structures. Most existing hypertext systems are set up as fixed information in the nodes as written by the original author. Some systems can generate nodes from code programmed or referenced by the author; a simple example would be retrieving a graphic in another location or pictures from a videodisc.

Access to information structures can be in the form of explicit links or implicit links. The typical link is explicit, because it provides an anchor at the departure point with a concrete object to click or otherwise activate, and because the pathway from anchor to destination is predefined by the author. Those systems that provide implicit links (e.g., dictionary lookup on the fly) depend upon properties of the information; only when the user makes a specific request does the system find a destination for the link. A third format for links, such as computed links (e.g. next-train schedules from an online tourist advisory), are pathways entirely determined while the user is in the system.

The use of annotations (small pop-up notes of hypertext) is one of the best ways to enhance learner control at the HAM level. The learner is permitted to 'customize' the pop-up window with an explanatory note or some supplemental facts or anything else that could be concisely expressed for perspective.

1.2.6 Major Systems

According to literature on the background of hypertext and hypermedia (Nielsen, 1990; Rada, 1991), NoteCards, designed at Xerox PARC, originally ran on Xerox Lisp computers in the powerful Interlisp programming environment. NoteCards therefore provides users with an interface to a programming language. Anyone knowing Lisp could potentially change any aspect of the notecards and implement special card types. The system is based on links that are entered as text characters, and link types are overviewed with different line patterns. The system is built on four kinds of objects:

- Each node is one notecard opened as a window. Simplest card forms are plain text or graphics but at least 50 have specialized data structures.
- Links are typed-in connections between cards. Links are displayed as a small link icon or a box with the title of the destination card. Link 'type' is a user-chosen label that typically describes how the content in the departure and destination card is related.
- The browser card contains a structural overview diagram of cards and links. Different link types are indicated by different line patterns. The overview is active, allowing users to edit nodes and links by operating on boxes and lines in the browser. The layout of the overview is updated by the system reflecting changes in the hypertext structure (adding or deleting nodes and links).
- FileBox is an object for hierarchical nesting of cards. Each notecard is listed in exactly one FileBox. The FileBox object is like a utility notecard; it can contain other FileBoxes or be linked-to from other cards.

HyperCard was originally created as a graphics programming environment and has many applications built in which are not related to hypertext. The innovative features of HyperCard are powered by HyperTalk, the built-in programming language of HyperCard, which is reasonable easy to learn. This is a general programming language, most effective for prototyping and testing graphic user interfaces, but not really suitable for large-scale productions or systems. Transforming it to a modern system language would require some fundamental changes: making it completely object-oriented, easier to maintain, and adding advanced-user features or multi-user access (Nielsen, 1990; Rada, 1991).

- The basic node object is the card (on the metaphor of a record card). A collection of cards is called a stack.
- HyperCard is mostly frame-based but scrolling text fields can be included in the content of a card.
- Links do not have to be hardwired because jumps are implemented as programming statements associated with buttons or fields.

- Hypertext support is through buttons, visible or hidden within other display components, which typically activate links when the user clicks on them. One of the flexible aspects is that links may be activated by events other than clicking, such as when the cursor passing over a region, while the mouse is held down, after an elapsed time period, etc.
- Pop-ups can be presented similar to those in Guide by authoring *show* or *hide* commands in buttons.
- A limitation for hypertext is that, unlike Guide, the format does not have 'sticky' buttons which latch onto text strings; hence, if users are allowed to edit the text the link button would not move with the text string but would stay in its original position on the screen.

Intermedia, as mentioned earlier, was a powerful hypertext system that ran under Unix. Intermedia was based on the scrolling window model but the essence of the Intermedia approach was a linking protocol defining the way other applications link to and from the system's documents. With this protocol in place, new and specialized hypertext applications could be written and readily integrated into the existing Intermedia applications; that is, present applications would already be able to interact with new ones (Nielsen, 1990; Rada, 1991).

Other basic aspects of Intermedia included:

- A document in Intermedia was created in a direct manipulation environment (i.e., with visual task representations); cutting and pasting can be done from one application to another.
- A block is defined as any information or material that the user selects within a document.
- One user-selection provides the source of a link, another selection determines the destination block; thus, a bi-directional link is created which can be followed in either direction. Keywords applied to links will allow the user to attach one or more attributes to the link. Paths can be defined as sequences of links.
- The keywords on links can be used to filter searches; only links with certain attributes would then be viewable.
- Views can be generated at the document–document, document–block, and block–block levels; different views can be generated dynamically by a user based on filtering criteria.
- The author of a presentation using a drawing package constructs overview documents; it is usually a convention that the overviews have a common layout.

Several other useful facilities are available including the animation editor InterPlay, the InterLex server for dictionary lookup, an InterNote annotation facility, and a full text search engine (Nielsen, 1990; Rada, 1991).

In 1990 Apple Computers, Inc. effectively put an end to the Intermedia project, part of which they had funded, by so altering A/UX, their version of UNIX, that all development of the program ceased.

1.2.7 Internet Systems with Hypertext or Hypermedia

Until 1991, using the Internet was telnet and ftp, strictly at the mercy of the remote system's peculiarities. Getting in was not difficult, since anonymous-user-ID, e-mail-address-password was standard, but finding the file and transferring it in the correct format was problematic. When a team of staff and students at the University of Minnesota developed Gopher, a collection of navigation tools built into simple collections of menus, they created the first on-line browser (Seiter & Negrino, 1995; Theise, 1995; Karpinski, 1996).

Gopher was parallel to hypertext systems in the sense that it was designed to be user-centered. When the user makes a selection from the menus, the Gopher client program sends a message to Gopher servers. Similar to a hypertext jump, the server sends back another menu, a requested document, or whatever information is needed to satisfy the request; also like a hypertext system, the client keeps track of where the user has been. As a PC-based file search-and-retrieval system Gopher (for the Mac, TurboGopher) rapidly grew into the basic Internet tool for obtaining information on the Internet. The total of all gopher resources available was referred to as "gopher space" (akin to hyperspace); in gopher space, archives are indexed, so a gopher search can find all sorts of files relatively efficiently.

Most people do not realize that the first version of the Web was entirely text-based, with hypertext links scattered throughout long passages of scientific literature. Hypertext technology is the foundation of the World Wide Web, with the intention that text and interface be designed to emulate human thinking. At the National Center for Supercomputing Applications (NCSA) in the early 1990s, a student named Marc Andreesen (later of Netscape) produced NCSA Mosaic, a creation which put the Web at the forefront of computing on the Internet. This earliest graphical browser was made ready for three platforms (Unix, Mac, and Windows) and then given away. Mosaic had a fun interface that encouraged the use of pictures and could be adapted to different modes of Internet access from dial-up to dedicated (Seiter & Negrino, 1995; Theise, 1995; Karpinski, 1996).

The framework of the present Web became complete with the introduction of HTML, the simple text-marking language for preparing Web documents. Simplicity is intentional because the idea is to have a document format that adapts to any computer so that it is displayed in a consistent manner. Dr. Tim Berners-Lee (formerly of the European physics research facility CERN, now at MIT) actually created HTML from the earlier document-formatting language SGML, which was a proven publishing format approach for book-length documents.

With the mainstream adoption of sophisticated, multiplatform browsers, the Web is becoming a giant, interactive hypermedia system. Web browsers can now present information similar to gopher, because browsers recognize the file protocols at ftp and gopher sites and adjust to the formats accordingly. After 1996, newcomers to the Internet will probably view ftp and gopher as historical relics. Hyperlinks (links) have become the key to utilizing the Web and its resources. Links can connect HTML documents with other pages on the Web, to points within the same document, or to other types of files such as graphics, video, and sound files.

1.2.8 Applications of Hypertext

With mainstream use of hypertext, individuals have found many creative ways to implement hypertext to enable streamlined use of collaborative materials:

- New forms of document or fiction. Interactive fiction (shared universe, same story from different points of view).
- Online manuals. Online documentation (no one likes manuals, just saving time reading them). Repair manuals.
- Large Volume Hypertext. (Vannevar Bush) What could not be selected was lost. New forms of online cataloging. Dictionaries reference (OED) (and show images and play sounds). Libraries.
- Computer science itself. Use for prototyping user interface for almost any other program. Software engineering. CASE (specification, implementation cycle). For operating systems (to find files etc.).
- Collaborative production.
- Authentication. Auditing (links back from the final statement to the sections of the documents that gave rise to it). Generalization of this.
- Trade shows, catalogs, advertising.

1.2.9 Basic Elements of Hypertext

Text markup is a technique for describing an information structure; in 'markup' special tags are embedded in the character stream to indicate structural features of a document such as paragraph and section boundaries, indentations, and headings (Hodges & Sasnett, 1990). SGML is a language for logical document structure, which allows marking up for logical structure and not physical presentation.

HTML is the *lingua franca* for publishing hypertext on the World Wide Web. It is a non-proprietary format based upon SGML, and can be created and processed by a wide range of tools. Extensible HyperText Markup Language (XHTML) is a family of current and future document types and modules that reproduce, subset, and extend HTML, reformulated in XML.

The HTML instructions, along with any text to which the instructions apply, are called an HTML element. The HTML instructions are in turn called tags, and look like <element_name>. This is simply the element name surrounded by left and right angle brackets. HTML documents are structured into two parts, the HEAD, and the BODY. Both of these are contained within the HTML element, this element simply denotes this as an HTML document.

The head contains information about the document that is not generally displayed with the document, such as its TITLE. The BODY contains the body of the text, and is where you place the document material to be displayed. Elements allowed inside the HEAD, such as TITLE, are not allowed inside the BODY, and vice versa.

Many elements can have arguments that pass parameters to the interpreter handling this element. These arguments are called attributes of the element.

For example, consider the element A, which marks a region of text as the beginning (or end) of a hypertext link. This element can have several attributes. One of them, HREF, specifies the hypertext document to which the marked piece of text is linked. To specify this in the tag for A you would write:

<A HREF="http://www.somewhere.ca/file.html"> *marked text* </a>.

where the attribute HREF is assigned the indicated value.

1.2.10 Authoring Hypertext

The authors of good hypertext systems create their wares according to the *3 golden rules of hypertext* (Nielsen, 1990):

1. A large body of information is to be organized into numerous fragments.
2. The fragments relate to each other.
3. The user needs only a small fraction at any time.

After inspecting these criteria, it hopefully is clear that not every knowledge-resource and learning application should be done using hypertext. For example, the author should never use hypertext if the application of knowledge requires the user to be away from the computer. In most situations of computer-based instruction or access, this caution is obviated by the actual presence of the user in front of the screen.

In Rada's (1991) subdivision of hypertext the distinguishing characteristics are directly related to the size of the application. Small-volume hypertext or microtext focuses on creating a single document with explicit links among its components; thus, a "microtext system" would manage a single document which is intended to be used in stand-alone interaction with one person. It seems plausible, however, to also think of a user-modified document, having a customized design of the learner's own choosing, as another kind of small-volume hypertext even if it is supported by a larger system.

By contrast, Rada states that large volume hypertext or macrotext must emphasize links among many different documents. Library collections are a perfect example of the knowledge base for a macrotext system. The relevant documents are from many different sources and an institution is to be involved in maintaining the system. System maintenance requires updating and evaluating both the interface to the documents and the connections (links) among documents. Multiple users of the established macrotext are searching for relatively few documents from a very large set. Strictly speaking, in this conceptualization, macrotext does not support the browsing of a single document, hence this would be performed by a helper microtext facility. The pre-eminent example of a macrotext is Xanadu, discussed previously.

In most libraries, at present, online indexing in terms of alphabetic subject, title and author categorization does not yet provide the essence of a macrotext system, although there is a significant advantage over cardfile predecessors in terms of speed. A large-volume hypertext system would require links through many texts supported entirely by electronic information storage and retrieval, with integrated archiving and indexing.

The function of hypertext is generally very similar to a database, and to expert systems as well (computer-based intelligent systems or artificial intelligence). Each of these systems accesses a knowledge base and retrieves/transmit information according to specified parameters. Nielsen (1990) explains that most hypertext systems are built from uniform hypertext engines that can display many kinds of hypertext documents. Hypertext engines are advantageous to authoring, because the author does not have to program a completely new application for every system and learners may already be familiar with the user interface. Still, having some flexibility is helpful for the experienced author and some hypertext engines allow the designer to customize the user interface to a document within a certain framework.

Hypertext documents can always be modified into special implementations by a skilled author; of particular importance for the potential of this technology is the implementation of various forms of multimedia presentation. Large (1996) points out that all multimedia implementations share two main characteristics: they simultaneously combine information in several media [text, still images, moving images (animation and video), and sound]; and they must be interactive, permitting users to call up information in any media as required and to flexibly navigate through a multimedia database often using hypertext structures.

- The content of a particular document or node should form a cohesive information structure; the quality of this structure determines the success of knowledge acquisition for that node, but also the effectiveness of links and other nodes. When writing hypertexts it is most effective to keep each node focused on a topic, and to present information in shorter segments, because absorbing knowledge from the computer screen is significantly slower than from paper (reading speed is about 30% slower from the screen).
- The author must always be critical of links (do not add too many) and their placement, especially with sophisticated users who have well-developed text comprehension and learning skills; they have to be convinced that the links are useful, not troublesome.
- Whenever users are moving around a large information space, as they can using hypertext, there is a real chance that they may get lost or not find the information they need (Nielsen, 1990).
- If lost in hyperspace, users must always know how to return to where the system started. As a general preventative strategy, the hypertext system would visually reveal "arrival" at the destination, and clearly relate the departure and destination by affirming why the link was chosen. Most frame-based hypertext systems use links that point to an entire node; but when the destination document is large it would be an advantage to more specifically fix the destination point and provide the user with precise arrival cues.

How else can we keep the learner from getting lost in the first place? Nielsen (1990) describes several possible solutions to the navigation problem:

- One obvious solution is to provide guided tours or 'trails', like a superlink through a series of nodes. This has advantages for new hypertext users or special interest users, especially if they can take side trips and then enter a single command to return to the trail point where the tour was suspended. The main disadvantage is that guided tours bring us back to linear sequencing; tours or trails simply cannot be the only navigation facility and still preserve an open learning hyperspace.
- Going backwards, the backtrack–history–bookmark approach, is available in some form on almost every hypertext system. History lists show all previously visited nodes, whereas the bookmark list contains

only nodes that the learner believes should be revisited. Other ideas include smart bookmarks that would provide some reorienting context after backtracking, and shopping-list bookmarks to accumulate references for nodes to be visited later.

- Overview diagrams are like maps of places to go, how to get there and back; some hypertext systems display both global and local overviews. Alternative methods might be a zoom facility to display more or less detail on command, or a 'fisheye' view showing more extensive information for nodes closer to the user's location with diminishing detail farther away. Marking the path traveled on a map, like footprints, enhances the map; furthermore, the author could also designate several high-connectivity nodes as special landmarks in the learning process.
- Providing contextual information like varying backgrounds and visual effects for different locations really addresses the homogeneity problem (all hypertext tends to look monotonously the same) but it also helps with the navigation problem.
- New control structures; the main hypertext control structure is a *goto* statement in the form of a jump, whereas an alternative would be an analogy to 'structured programming', such as the nested hierarchies in the hypertext system Guide. Another example of a structured hypertext mechanism is link inheritance applied to overview diagrams; instead of showing detailed links between all nodes, any related clusters of nodes in a hierarchy are linked to other clusters or nodes with a single inheritance line (link).
- It is obviously not feasible to one-jump navigate everywhere in a massive hyperspace. The answer is to apply some search mechanism through the use of queries. A full text search finds incidences of a word/phrase specified by the user; one useful method is a menu display of all hits and number of hits on a node. Search results can also be added to overview diagrams by highlighting nodes that were hit and annotating node labels with the frequencies. More sophisticated programs for information retrieval might evaluate the similarity of available nodes to the requested information in terms of a query score. This might be a sum of the number of hits on a node (an intrinsic score of how well the node matches the query) and a weighted average of contiguous nodes (an extrinsic score of how well other nodes it is linked to match the query). The result could be a 'filtered' hypertext of only relevant nodes which is easier to navigate and simpler to display in overview diagrams.

1.2.11 Usability and Intelligent Hypertext

According to Nielsen (1990), evaluating the usability of a hypertext system is based on five concerns:

1. Is the system easy to learn?
2. Is the system efficient in terms of productivity?
3. Is it easy to remember how the system works?
4. Is it typical to make few errors?
5. Is the system pleasant to use?

A single guiding principle of usability, which underlies each of these concerns, is to design an interface which keeps the user informed with precise, relevant, and understandable feedback about what the system is doing.

As suggested earlier, hypertext systems share some commonalties with expert systems. Rada (1991) tells us that expert systems are designed to directly solve problems, yet they also involve transmitting important information from an expert to the learner. Likewise, in a hypertext system the author is communicating with the learner through textual information structures. The two kinds of systems can be enhanced through a synergistic combination of both, which is described as an expertext system or intelligent hypertext.

Hypertext can be integrated with an expert system so that the expert system can (synergistically) better explain its decisions. Textbook information can be offered to the user when the expert system is questioned. From the other side, the links in hypertext may be difficult to follow. Hypertext systems can include expert system features that help the user find relevant information (Rada, 1991, p. 145).

What intelligent hypertext offers, then, is the opportunity to achieve the full "potential for an author (researcher/designer) to establish a network of interconnected nodes of information for the purpose of supporting users' exploration of a problem space ..." (Harland, 1989).

1.3 Multimedia

1.3.1 Multimedia Authoring

What is multimedia? The American Heritage Dictionary defines it as "the combined use of several media, such as movies, slides, music, and lighting, especially for the purpose of education or entertainment."

The term *authoring* refers to "programming by non-programmers". Creating media-enhanced pages used to be the domain of the desktop publishing specialist. Although there are professional web designers, many now chose to go it alone and be talented amateurs.

Creation of media for entertainment, education, or in the case of industry, informational marketing, can take many forms. For the sake of discussion, we are concerned with interactive multimedia, the use of varied media in combination with computer technology. This marriage creates an especially effective method of presenting information. By using interactivity to involve the user, more knowledge is retained, far more than the rate for most other instructional methods. Forms of interactive multimedia include Web sites, CD-ROMs, programs, presentations, tutorials, help sections, and even games.

The term *multimedia* is sometimes used interchangeably with hypermedia, although a subtle distinction applies. Romiszowski (1993) argues that multimedia is the concept of using a variety of media to improve the instruction of a particular topic, whereas hypermedia refers to storage of information in a network such that the information in one media source can be easily cross-referenced to relevant information in another source. In a hypermedia system the linkages are handled as data which can be searched or manipulated collectively, but this is not a requirement for multimedia designs (Hodges & Sasnett, 1990).

What exactly is it attempting to accomplish? According to Hodges and Sasnett (1990), the growth of multimedia computing is proceeding along two loci of change. The first is in the technical requirements of multimedia as a fusion of data types, combining and managing text with graphics, video and audio. The second locus of change is a fusion of different modes of expression to fit human symbolic capacities; what tools will allow us to draw upon the full spectrum of expressive possibilities with a minimum of training or difficulty?

The result for the learner is a new learning environment in which theory and experiences can be explored concurrently. Realistic simulations are possible: for example, imagine a how-to course on sailing with tutorial lessons, video interaction, nautical charts and guides linked together with a single method of cross-referencing (Hodges & Sasnett, 1990). From an authoring perspective this involves folding and unfolding files as needed. A reference button may be used to jump elsewhere to display additional material and fire up other media; and the process of inlining may be used to break up large scenes into separate files that can be loaded one at a time, which allows the learner to begin viewing a scene immediately rather than waiting for a large file to download (Karpinski, 1996).

From the view of Karpinski (1996), Web authoring is being transformed rapidly in a revolution beyond basic inline data types (text and graphics) to a variety of multimedia and interactive content. Even more promising is the growth of executable content in which Web browsers download and run mini-applications (called applets) so that Web pages will behave more and more like desktop programs. These possibilities are due to the emerging 'plug-in architecture' of browsers that was pioneered by Netscape. [A detail not mentioned in the Karpinski article is that at least one of the applications mentioned, ToolVox, will probably use the proposed real-time transfer standard (RTP) since it is from a vendor acquired by Netscape as part of its LiveMedia solution, which uses RTP.]

Frylinck and Raitt (1993) believe that libraries, whether public, special, or educational, should be effective purveyors of interactive multimedia (IMM). The use of IMM holds many opportunities for dynamic and appealing user information systems:

- A growing number of publishers are placing reference works on CD-ROM and optical cards.
- Smart cards, with write-once or erasable technology, could allow book editions without printing.
- Canadian Smart Library Project: the goal is access to electronic information in all media anywhere in the world; uses optical card technology for security.
- Idea of IMM resources stored in central electronic libraries to be called up as required by subscribers [Bell Atlantic and AT&T have begun a project to allow sound and full-motion video across telephone lines using ADSL technology (recall the conclusion of Online Services notes!)].
- Virtual Reality: when costs decline, may have virtual access for users, training for library staff.
- State Library of New South Wales, Australia: ISDN telecommunications technology demonstrates feasibility of transferring multimedia images scanned from collections in one library to another.
- Australian Telelibrary Project: developing a system for electronic scanning, storage, retrieval, and delivery of full text documents and images.
- Project Gutenberg: attempts to support the creation and distribution of electronic books; more than one patron can use at a time; computer-searchable collections which could be transmitted by discs, telephone lines, or other media.

1.3.2 Multimedia in Internet

A great deal of information on the Internet is stored in text format. There are full text articles, electronic journals, books, novels, Internet guides, computer software manuals, computer standards, and government documents, but to name a few. To utilize this, web designers either create pages in HTML, have plug-ins such as Adobe Acrobat or Microsoft Word, or link users to download documents in their original format, such as PostScript.

Common Gateway Interface (CGI) is a standard method of extending Web server functionality by executing programs or scripts on a Web server in response to Web browser requests. One common use is form processing.

Another approach is to have embedded media in an HTML or XML document. There are various kinds of embedded media:

Plug-ins

Plug-ins are programs which run within the web browser, and are called when certain types of data are loaded. For example, a plug-in is available enabling Macromedia's Shockwave (a web-based multimedia environment derived from Macromedia Director) files to be run. When the web browser loads the Shockwave file, the plug-in is automatically called to display it.

External applications

One of the compelling things about the World Wide Web is its multimedia nature – it easily includes graphics, sounds, and even video. While the details of working with these formats is beyond the scope of this brief note, there are several important points to keep in mind.

Graphics can be very valuable and make it possible to communicate things that would be very difficult to do with text, but though a picture may be worth a thousand words, it may take ten times longer to download and display. Keep in mind also that some of your readers will be using text-only browsers or will have automatic image loading disabled or may be using screen readers or Braille output devices, so use graphics judiciously and provide a text alternative where possible.

When including graphical content be sure to use the *alt* attribute of the *img* tag when appropriate. This allows users with text-only browsers and users with automatic image loading disabled to still use your pages. Use the *alt* text to convey the same information that the image would have provided (as far as that is possible).

When designing, one should try to accommodate a wide range of client hardware – older, slower machines, monitors of various sizes and color capability, etc. Also consider the range of network connectivity possibilities from fast Ethernet to slow dial-up SLIP and PPP connections.

Graphical web browsers like Netscape Navigator support two kinds of graphics. Inline images appear on your web page, intermingled with your text. External images are displayed in a separate window and may use an external application as a viewer. There are advantages and disadvantages to each method. Inline graphics are limited to the formats supported by the browser (GIF is most common, JPEG nearly so, and PNG is supported by later browser versions) and large images might cause problems, but no additional software is needed. External images may mean that the readers of your page must have software in addition to a web browser (but that is not unlikely) and their workstation may need additional memory. But an external viewing application may support more file formats (GIF, JPEG, TIFF, and PICT are very common), handle large images more gracefully, and may have other features. Whether to use an external application or not to view an external image is often under the control of the individual browser configuration.

Except for exceptional situations it is best to restrict yourself to GIF and JPEG images. GIF is better for non-photographic elements and for situations that can work well with the 256-color limit of the format. GIF also supports interleaved images, improving the perceived speed of the rendering of your page, and transparent images. JPEG is better for photographic images and situations requiring more than 256 colors. JPEG is a lossy format – it compresses the image by removing detail – and that may or may not be acceptable depending on the application. GIF is a lossless format. Newer browsers support progressive JPEG images, which are similar to interleaved GIF images. Newer browsers also support PNG images, which is a lossless format designed for web applications.

When designing your images you should use 72 dpi to match or at least approximate the resolution of most monitors, which commonly range from the 60s to the 90s. GIF and JPEG are simple, bitmap image formats that do not include size or resolution information.

If a color specified isn't available a similar color may be substituted or dithering may be used to approximate it. Some image editing software can convert an image to use a 256-color palette that is likely to be available on a variety of platforms and browsers. Another useful technique is to use a small inline image (called a thumbnail) as a link to a larger external image. An inline image can be used as a link to another page and can be mapped to contain active areas that are links to multiple pages.

For sounds, the major consideration here is the trade-off between file size and sound quality. Browser plug-in modules, such as the QuickTime plug-in available for Netscape Navigator, plays sounds in several formats. Some browsers, and older versions of Netscape, may not have this capability and will require external applications to play sound files. Support for MPEG audio is also widely available. AIFF and WAV are platform-dependent and should be avoided. Support via browser plug-ins is also becoming available for MIDI (Musical Instrument Digital Interface) files. When appropriate, MIDI can allow higher quality sound for music with relatively small files.

There is also a trade-off when it comes to video. It is also possible to include video clips in your pages, with support from browser plug-ins and external applications. MPEG is the most widely supported format, followed by QuickTime. As you might expect, video files are very large and the size/quality trade-off is even more problematic. For example, a file size of size of 1Mb Video takes 10 minutes to download with an analogue connection.

Scripts (Visual Basic, Java)
JavaScript is a scripting language. Although similar in some ways to Java, it is not a complete programming language, but is designed to be easier to use and accessible to anyone who can write HTML. It is specifically aimed at enhancing web pages. Unlike Java, it is not compiled, but interpreted by the browser, like HTML, so JavaScript can be embedded directly into HTML files. It should be noted that a Java-enabled web browser will not necessarily be JavaScript enabled, and vice-versa.

ActiveX and ActiveX Controls
ActiveX was developed by Microsoft, and is based on their OLE (object linking and embedding) technology. In many ways it represents existing Microsoft technology bundled to work over the Internet. It is not a programming language, but rather a set of rules for how applications should share information. Unlike Java, it is platform-dependent, and therefore currently restricted to users running Internet Explorer or Netscape Navigator with the ActiveX plug-in, though a beta version is also available for the Macintosh. An ActiveX control is similar to a Java applet, but has a much greater access to the operating system, providing more flexibility but at a cost of decreased security.

ActiveX is about providing the highest level of support for the latest HTML standards used on the Web. ActiveX also incorporates the other core Internet standards such as HTTP and NNTP network protocols.

ActiveX Scripting allows multiple controls to be fully integrated into complete applications. Scripting refers to the use of a high-level programming language, such as Visual Basic script or JavaScript, to automate and integrate the behaviors of controls, documents, Web browsers, and Web Servers. For example, scripting can be used in an audio control when the user pushes a push-button control.

ActiveX Documents allow the Web browser to also browse contents defined in other formats. Application supporting ActiveX Documents can have their documents be activated, browsed, and edited directly within the browser in this manner, making it easier for the user to use a wide variety of published information on the web and corporate Intranets. ActiveX supports leading-edge multimedia standards like Open Type fonts, a wide variety of media formats for playback of audio, video and animation over low bandwidth connections.

Macromedia Shockwave and Flash

Macromedia's Shockwave and Flash products have changed the face of the Web by enabling designers to incorporate interactive animations and sounds in their pages. The emergence of "Shocked" technologies has led to a new level of interactivity on the Web, from gaming, to marketing, to the presentation of news stories. To take advantage of Shockwave- or Flash-based content, the browser must have either the Shockwave or Shockwave Flash plug-in installed.

To view movies over the Internet, WAV and MIDI files can also be put into Web pages, but users should have a capable browser, such as:

- Video for Windows – AVI
- Apple QuickTime – MOV
- Motion Picture Experts Group – MPEG.

Introduction to Streaming Video

Streaming video may be used for live or recorded events. The main reason for broadcasting live is to reach a wider and/or more dispersed audience. Typical live broadcasts could be lectures, sports or entertainment events, and academic or other ceremonies. For a major academic lecture given at a university the number of people who could actually attend would be limited by the size of the lecture theatre, whilst the potential audience could be anywhere in the world.

If an event is broadcast live it is relatively simple to make a recording which can then be published on the Web for later viewing. However, there are many more possibilities with non-live broadcasts. A streamed broadcast should be considered to be a multimedia event, which could include full-motion video if appropriate. Good examples of multimedia lectures can be found at the Boxmind site <http://www.boxmind.com/>. Boxmind use synchronized broadcasts with several streams containing video, audio, scrolling text, pictures or diagrams, and hypertext links.

Streaming video provides a continuous stream of information that is transmitted, and receivers are able to tune in and receive the information in real time. Streaming across the Internet, although similar in concept, has its own specific issues that must be addressed. The Internet was not designed for real-time streaming. The Internet is a shared medium and uses a best effort delivery mechanism, Internet Protocol (IP), to deliver content. There is no dedicated path between source and the sink. IP breaks content up into self-contained packets and these packets are routed independently. Limited bandwidth, latency, noise, packet loss, retransmission and out-of-order packet delivery are all problems that can affect real-time streaming over the Internet.

Live or on-demand streaming is a time-critical application that is sensitive to the variation in delay that is normal for a shared-access network like the Internet. Not only does the amount of bandwidth that you have access to matter but also the consistency or quality of this bandwidth. All Internet streaming technologies get around this by buffering a certain amount of content before actually starting to play.

The buffer irons out the natural traffic variations inherent on the Internet. Many seconds worth of content can be buffered and in excess of 30 seconds worth is not uncommon. Note that after the initial buffering the streamed broadcast will start to play at the same time as more content is being downloaded. This is an improvement over earlier technologies where the whole file had to be downloaded before playing could commence.

But the majority of international end users are still accessing the Internet over very narrowband dial-up links. Comparatively few people have the luxury of access at anything over 2Mbps, however over the last couple of years cable and DSL access has been increasing allowing bandwidths between 128kbps and 512kbps to be available to end users. At this bit rate near-VHS-quality rich media can be achieved through modern compression techniques and sophisticated codec technology. It is not all about quality of bandwidth however. Content creation, serving, usability and availability are also challenges that need to be addressed.

Standard Compression Technologies

There are a variety of compression systems used today. The Motion Picture Experts Group (MPEG) has three open (ISO/IEC) standards that can be used for streaming. Their MPEG-1, MPEG-2, MPEG-4, MPEG-7, and MPEG-21 standards have been used in VCD, HDTV, DVD and DTV. MPEG is capable of compressing the video digital data to between one-fortieth and one-fiftieth of its original size. For example, a one-hour movie compressed to one-fiftieth of its original size requires two gigabytes. A two-hour movie needs four gigabytes, which is the exact storage size of a DVD disk. For Internet transmission, one needs far greater compression.

The vision for MPEG-21 is to define a multimedia framework to enable transparent and augmented use of multimedia resources across a wide range of networks and devices.

Proprietary Compression Solutions – The Big Three

- Real Networks – RealOne Player: A very popular player, which is very widely distributed and available for all major OS platforms.

RealNetworks claim over 70% of the Internet streaming market with the player being installed on over 90% of home PCs. They offer media creation and management tools, as well as the Audio and Video players. RealPlayer is now called RealOne Player and the latest generation codecs (developed with Intel), coupled with their SureStream technology, will probably keep them in a dominant position. SureStream is an automatic multi-bit-rate technology that will adjust the streamed data rate to suit the client's connectivity. In practical terms this means that a single encoding will suit all users from dial-up to corporate LAN. Also supported is Synchronized Multimedia Integration Language (SMIL) which allows mixed multimedia content to be delivered in a synchronized way.

- QuickTime: Originally developed in 1991, with QuickTime 5 reaching over 100 million Mac and PC users in its first year alone, the introduction of MPEG-4 allows QuickTime to define its future within digital media. QuickTime's major advantages are its maturity and the large number of codecs available for it. It features an open plug-in feature to allow third party codecs to be added. MPEG-1 and MPEG-4 codecs are currently available. The plug-in feature has allowed over 200 digital media formats to be supported by QuickTime 4 with companies such as Sorenson Labs producing very impressive codecs. As with RealPlayer, SMIL is available and now RTSP is also supported. (Prior to version 4 only progressive streaming, not true real-time streaming, was available in QuickTime). QuickTime server is supported natively in MAC OS. The open source Darwin Streaming Server is available for other platforms and is free.
- Windows Media Player (currently at version 9, launched in the fall of 2002) is the newcomer to the streaming world. Windows Media Player 9, formerly code-named Corona, has been in development for nearly four years at a cost of about $500 million, Gates said. It improves on earlier versions of Microsoft's digital player and server technology on a number of fronts. For businesses, the technology includes improved media management features. For consumer media playing, the system is updated for speed and seamless playback to create a more TV-like experience on the PC.

  Microsoft's streaming server (called Microsoft Media Services) is free and supplied as standard under Windows 2000 Server and as a free download for Windows NT/2000 server. Microsoft have not open-sourced the code which means that other platforms are not supported. This is considered a major disadvantage as far as flexibility is concerned.

The Streaming Model

The components of an end-to-end streaming system are the client or player, the server and some sort of content creation process. There are various production tools to create the content. These tools convert audio, video, or animation to a data-type format that the server can stream. Because most servers can deliver content in many different formats, there are a number of tools that people can use in creating content. Production tools can epitomize the content for efficient delivery over the Internet, based on the nature of the material and the capabilities of the client computers.

RealNetwork's RealProducer 8 will convert from a number of raw formats (AVI, MPEG-1, AU, AIFF etc.) and is free for the basic version. Apple's QuickTime Player (free and pro) also provides content authoring and import/export facilities and Media On-Demand Producer is free from Microsoft.

Streaming Servers

Just as a Web server delivers pages to Web browsers over the Internet, streaming servers deliver media clips to clients (clips are created with the production tools described elsewhere). Real-time streaming requires specific servers.

RealNetworks, Microsoft and Apple all provide streaming servers. These servers give you a greater level of control over your media delivery but can be more complicated to set up and administer than a standard HTTP server. Also, real-time streaming uses special network protocols, such as RTSP or MMS (Microsoft Media Server). Microsoft envisions Windows Media Series 9 as a way for third parties to deliver and sell digital content services, whether streamed or downloaded.

Ideally the user should have a simple hypertext interface and have to do no more than click on a link. Any upgrade or download of a client player utility should be automated and transparent. In practice client downloads tend to be large and complicated procedures with too many options available for the average user.

Streaming availability on the global Internet should ideally mean a server ready to stream content to any clients who have an interest in receiving it. Unfortunately the demand and availability of media-rich content has lead to a breakdown of the traditional client–server model. Single servers streaming content to diverse groups of clients distributed across the Internet are ineffective in terms of both server load and network congestion.

Content Delivery Networks (CDN)

Over the last couple of years strategies have evolved in the commercial sector to address these problems. Content Delivery Networks (CDNs) are an attempt to introduce a coherent approach to building an infrastructure of caching proxies, mirror servers and proxy accelerators to enable a more efficient and speedier delivery of streamed content to end users. The ultimate goal is to replicate content and bring it closer to the end user in a transparent fashion. In this way the user sees no URL changes and has no knowledge (nor interest) in the actual source of the content. Examples you may have heard of are:

- Akamai with its FreeFlow technology
- Digital Island with its Footprint technology.

Network Demand

The nature of the Internet and its use of IP means that a broadcast is competing with other data transmissions, and in general there is no way of guaranteeing sufficient bandwidth to ensure an uninterrupted broadcast. Video conferencing systems usually use other network technologies such as ISDN, which has a relatively low but guaranteed end-to-end bandwidth, or ATM that can be set up with channels with guaranteed Quality of Service (QoS). Bandwidth over the Internet is increasing rapidly but unfortunately demand seems to be keeping up with supply, so increasing bandwidth alone is unlikely to solve the problem.

Various developments are taking place which should ultimately result in guaranteed Quality of Service (QoS) being available over IP and this, together with the emergence of CDNs, should result in a rapid growth in the use of video over the Internet.

Because 'live' broadcasts are not really live but are typically delayed for around 30 seconds it is difficult to set up remote feedback. For example, where an on-line lecture has been publicized in advance, it would be beneficial to allow questions from the remote audience. One way to achieve this would be to set up a Web page so that people could type in their questions, which could then to relayed to the lecturer by another person in the room.

Although easy to produce, a continuous shot of someone talking direct to camera is technically demanding on bandwidth and probably adds relatively little to the presentation. In particular, when producing material for education and training a combination of slide shows, animation and recorded computer session together with a commentary is easier to deliver and in many cases more effective than full-motion video.

1.4 Case Study: Boxmind.com

Figure 1.9. Example of Boxmind.com (Acknowledgements to Eurovestech plc)

Boxmind Limited is the Oxford, UK-based media publisher, software house and online education consultancy, bringing together world-famous academics and entrepreneurs to create an electronic educational standard for the 21st century.

Boxmind has produced and holds rights in perpetuity to 39 e-lectures by some of the world's most eminent academics including Michael Beloff, QC, Professor Richard Dawkins, Professor Niall Ferguson, Professor Susan Greenfield, Professor Germaine Greer, Professor John Kay, Sir Martin Rees and Nobel prize winner, Amartya Sen.

Boxmind's founders, Richard Halkett (CEO), David Auckland and Richard Comish (CTO), all graduates from Oxford University, have been working closely with an editorial board of internationally renowned academics consisting of Richard Dawkins, John Kay, Peter Atkins and David Womersley. Boxmind's authoring software and content, the former enabling academic institutions and corporates to produce their own e-lectures within networked environments, is in strong demand not only from its target market of universities and corporates, but also from local education authorities, city learning centers, city technology centers and schools. The individual market is being pursued through partnerships.

In this rapidly expanding 'webucation' marketplace, Boxmind is seeking to position itself not in competition with existing institutions developing 'virtual' offerings, but as an essential support service for them, presiding over the best resources available online.

Questions:

1. Why would remote education be of value to possible students?
2. What are the strengths and limitations of remote learning via Boxmind?
3. What kind of support might a student need in using Boxmind?

1.5 Case Study: Open hypermedia for software project management

Software engineering solutions need to be able to handle the application and document heterogeneity of software development, provide principles and tools to capture implicit relationships (making them explicit) and automate the management of these relationships in order to address the scalability demands of large-scale projects. Open hypermedia is one such approach which has been used to address the complexity and heterogeneity of large-scale software development.

Open hypermedia possesses two key characteristics: externally managed relationships and third-party application integration. By providing techniques to integrate hypermedia into existing applications, a development organization is not forced to give up familiar applications or business processes when adopting open hypermedia.

The process of sorting through relevant materials and organizing them to meet the needs of the task at hand has been described as *information triage* (Marshall & Shipman, 1997). Managers not only read multiple project reports, but they do so *in parallel* in an attempt to uncover potential conflicts and shared interests between projects; Adler *et al.* (1998) have previously reported the frequent occurrence of this practice in work-related reading. The 'working document' is not available to any staff other than the authoring manager (being stored on the local machine rather than in the report repository), which makes it difficult for managers to share their notes and comments or collaborate on the production of a summary report (such communication currently takes place over e-mail, which leaves no record connected to the document that such a discussion has taken place).

Process of transition

Organizations are keen to move away from the ad-hoc shared 'report repositories' towards an (intranet) Web-based environment, with improved, structured, access to project reports. Managers and staff would continue to use Microsoft Word as their preferred tool for report composition, but would publish these reports on the Web.

The use of a standard Web-based infrastructure (that is, Web servers and browsers) to publish material on the corporate intranet renders the published information read-only. With knowledge and 'ownership' of Web server space, anyone can compose and publish new information on the Web, and can link their contribution to any other Web document (without having to own it). However, the information repository essentially remains unalterable (and hence 'read-only').

Publishing on the Web (or Web-based environments) is characterized by the addition of new content – authors cannot modify existing content. By contrast, a company's management reporting activity is not entirely characterized by the composition of new (original) material. IT managers annotate and collate relevant information from multiple sources (including latest project status reports, previous status reports, and summary reports) which forms the basis of new content presenting this information according to a different set of constraints.

'Open' hypermedia is about hypertext which is not confined to the boundaries of a single system, be it Web browser, text editor, video streamer or MIDI player. An open hypertext system achieves this openness or extensibility through a 'link service' or (more generally) 'structure service', which undertakes the management and deployment of the hypertext links independently of the documents or data which are being interconnected. Although the Web was developed largely independently of the research in open hypermedia systems at the time, the ubiquity of the Web along with the problems inherent in its design has motivated researchers to retro-fix their systems to it (Maurer, 1995; Carr *et al.*, 1995; Anderson, 1997; Bouvin, 1999), enhancing the functionality of the Web via a structure service to enable a 'Linkable Web'. Information in Web pages is distributed across the Web, connected by HTML links. Semantic Web research strives to augment this global information network with machine-understandable metadata in order that software as well as human agents can 'understand' it (Berners-Lee *et al.*, 2001); this metadata is distributed across the Web, and must also be interlinked.

One recent technique to address web scalability is reported with Chimera (Anderson, 1999). Chimera has the ability to import and export hypermedia information in XML (Bray, 1998). One industrial user leveraged this feature by creating parsers for several key artifact types. These parsers scan project artifacts for implicit anchor and link instances and then produce XML files containing information about the discovered anchors and links. Using this technique, over 500,000 anchors and links were created after scanning more than 30,000 pages of project artifacts. An interesting side-effect of the XML import/export files is that they facilitate the configuration management of hypermedia information.

Questions:

1. Why would a company be deterred from using Open Hypermedia?
2. How could sharing of information via open hypermedia change organizational interactions?

1.6 Key Terms

Human Computer Interaction (HCI): The study of how people interact with computers and to what extent computers are or are not developed for successful interaction with human beings. One important HCI factor is that different users form different conceptions or mental models about their interactions and have different ways of learning and keeping knowledge and skills (different 'cognitive styles' as in, for example, 'left-brained' and 'right-brained' people). In addition, cultural and national differences play a part. Another consideration in studying or designing HCI is that user interface technology changes rapidly, offering new interaction possibilities to which previous research findings may not apply.

Hypertext: Hypertext is the organization of information units into connected associations that a user can choose to make. Ted Nelson first used the term in describing his Xanadu system.

Multimedia: Multimedia is more than one concurrent presentation medium (for example, on CD-ROM or a Web site). Although still images are a different medium than text, multimedia is typically used to mean the combination of text, sound, and/or motion video. Some people might say that the addition of animated images (for example, animated GIF on the Web) produces multimedia, but it has typically meant one of the following:

- Text and sound
- Text, sound, and still or animated graphic images
- Text, sound, and video images
- Video and sound
- Multiple display areas, images, or presentations presented concurrently
- In live situations, the use of a speaker or actors and 'props' together with sound, images, and motion video.

Multimedia can arguably be distinguished from traditional motion pictures or movies both by the scale of the production (multimedia is usually smaller and less expensive) and by the possibility of audience interactivity or involvement (in which case, it is usually called interactive multimedia). Interactive elements can include: voice command, mouse manipulation, text entry, touch screen, video capture of the user, or live participation (in live presentations).

Open hypermedia: Hypermedia, a term derived from hypertext, extends the notion of the hypertext link to include links among any set of multimedia objects, including sound, motion video, and virtual reality. It can also connote a higher level of user/network interactivity than the interactivity already implicit in hypertext. Open hypermedia is an approach to text relationship management and information organization that is characterized by three key features: external links, third-party application integration, and sophisticated hypermedia data models.

1.7 Review Questions

1. How has the evolution of HCI impacted the use of computers in the workplace?
2. What primary user interface issues should one consider in designing a systems for a wide variety of user groups?
3. How has hypertext changed the process of how one views a document?
4. Explain the three golden rules of hypertext, and how authoring hypertext depends on the size of the application.
5. Describe how multimedia is related to hypertext.

Chapter 2

GROUPS AND COLLABORATIVE TECHNOLOGY

Introduction

Moving towards a view of the entire corporation, the group is the next unit of analysis outwards from the individual. In order for groups of individuals to work together, there has to be both methods and tools (including technology) for collaboration to occur. We provide an overview of some of the methods currently used in industry, and discuss why place and time, fit and function, and application and motivation are all elements of a successful collaboration system.

Learning Objectives of the Chapter

When you have completed this chapter, you should be able to:

- Discuss collaborative principles for group systems
- Understand the history of groupware, and why certain approaches have enjoyed success more than others
- Advise on which systems is appropriate for a particular group work activity.

2.1 Collaborative Systems and Principles

The emergence and widespread adoption of the World Wide Web (WWW) offers a great deal of potential for the developers of collaborative technologies, both as an enabling infrastructure and a platform for integration with existing end-user environments.

What are collaborative systems? Also sometimes called groupware, Malone *et al.* (1992) define them as "information technology used to help people work together more effectively," implying, perhaps, that this new area is simply trying to take collaboration more seriously than traditional computer science fields.

Lynch, Snyder, and Vogel (1990) hint at what is missing in traditional fields: "Groupware is distinguished from normal software by the basic assumption it makes: groupware makes the user aware that he is part of the group, while most other software seeks to hide and protect users from each other."

Ellis *et al.* (1991) further qualify this definition, requiring also the common task criteria: "Groupware are computer-based systems that supports groups of people engaged in a common task (or goal) and that provide an interface to a shared environment." Peter and Trudy Johnson-Lenz are credited by many as coining the term groupware in 1978. Their definition of 'groupware' does not require that the tasks be associated with clear goals. They define groupware as "computer-mediated culture, intentional group processes plus supporting software," thus focussing on collaborative applications' ability to mediate the interaction among its users.

Electronic Meeting System (EMS) is yet another term introduced to distinguish software programs within the larger category of groupware. This term – introduced by Jay Nunamaker, a professor at the University of Arizona – is simply a network of PCs used to improve the communication and decision making that takes place in a traditional same-time/same-place or synchronous meeting (Weatherall and Nunamaker, 1996).

But where have we come from to get to what we now see as groupware? There are other technologies that have been tried and, to some extent, still somewhat succeed at enabling collaboration. "Somewhat succeed" in that they provide the tools, but not necessarily an agreed-upon collaboration methodology in their system.

Designing technology support for Group Work has been one of the driving forces behind what Tim Berners-Lee calls the "Semantic Web".

> "The Semantic Web is an extension of the current web in which information is given well-defined meaning, better enabling computers

and people to work in cooperation." – Tim Berners-Lee, James Hendler, Ora Lassila, The Semantic Web, *Scientific American,* May 2001.

In 1995, at one of the earlier meetings on WWW and collaborative systems, the following segmentation was given to types of collaboration systems that existed at that time:

- Real-time Systems: WebTalk with 'live' conferences on the Web
- Groupware Systems: e.g. InterNotes, collective filtering
- Shared Information Spaces: e.g. BSCW shared workspace system where you can have a shared collective disk space
- Group Knowledge: Semantics of open collaboration
- Annotation Systems: Shared commenting, rating systems, etc.

As one can see from the segmentation, part of the issue is not just the physical mechanism for collaboration, but the shared vision of methods of sharing and collaborating that address the successful continued use of the technology.

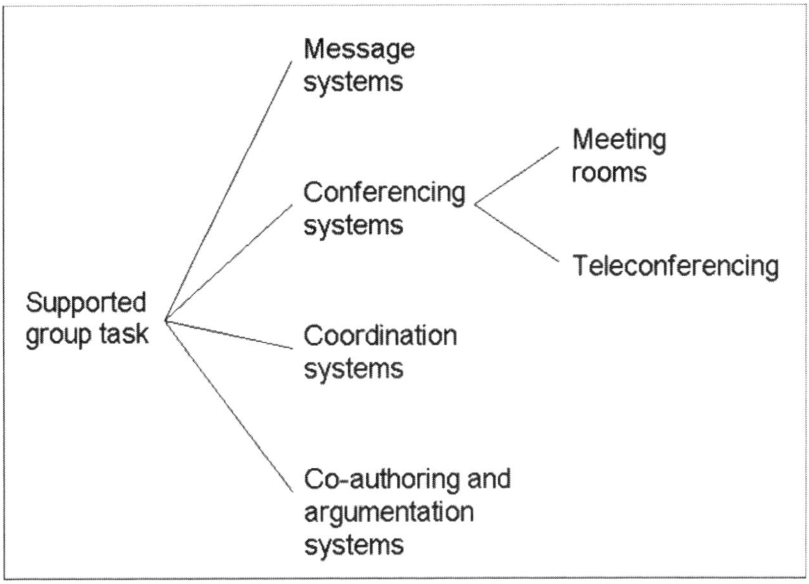

Figure 2.1 Segmentation of supported group tasks

2.1.1 Messaging Systems

In recent years, e-mail systems in most organizations have evolved into business critical operations. However, these systems are increasingly complex with organizations investing heavily in multiple-vendor e-mail solutions running on different platforms and protocols. To allow the exchange of messages between these different e-mail systems, additional hardware and software must be installed and managed, users must be retrained and administrators must focus on the time-consuming task of manually updating numerous mail directories to keep them synchronized.

Messaging systems handle the system translation and communication so that users can communicate transparently between virtually any type of PC, midrange, mainframe or Internet e-mail system wherever they reside. Utilizing a single, easy addressing scheme, users send and receive messages, including file attachments, through their familiar e-mail applications. Users can switch between e-mail platforms or change e-mail IDs without other users noticing. This transparent interoperability enables improved teamwork as well as global, corporate communications. Users also can exchange complex messages via the Internet or corporate intranets through messaging systems support of the Multipurpose Internet Mail Extension (MIME) protocol.

Why messaging systems have become so mission-critical to organizations and why they work comes down to the process methodology. Again, the user only has to know the name address of the fellow user, not the location of the mailbox nor the type of system used to access mail. The complexity is taken care of by the technology, not by the semantics of using the system. Messaging systems maintain a single corporate directory that allows users to view and utilize all other user e-mail addresses from within their own e-mail system. Directory synchronization as a technology function:

- enables system administrators to keep their local directories up to date
- automatically with the central directory
- allows local directories to include all, or a subset, of the central directory
- supports X.500 directory capabilities so that administrators can consolidate multiple e-mail directories into a single, easily accessible directory.

2.1.2 Conferencing Systems

Developers of virtual conferences attempt to create a stimulating and supportive learning environment without forcing participants to congregate at a particular location or time. Differentiating which human communication needs can be met at a distance through technology from those that can only be accomplished in face-to-face interaction is a continuing challenge. The virtual conference is designed both to provide a supportive context in which to develop our interpersonal skills and to enhance our understanding of mediated communication. The conference can be held either in real-time (synchronously) or with delays. The benefits of both types are listed in the Figure 2.2 below.

Asynchronous Interaction	Synchronous Interaction
• Freedom of time, so that learners participate when, and if, they choose	• Immediacy
• Time for reflection	• Faster problem solving, scheduling and decision making
• Opportunities to research and backup one's assertions	• Increased opportunities for developing affect
• Allows global communication, unbounded by time zone constraints	• Better for conference parties
• Greater anonymity and potential lack of responsibility by individual users	

Figure 2.2. Benefits of different times of interaction in virtual conferencing

2.1.3 Intelligent Agent Systems

There are various types of intelligent agents; ones for monitoring, ones for filtering, shopbots, artificial lifeforms, and many others. What they all have in common, in terms of collaboration, is a set of predefined rules and business processes they are governed by, set up by a user or user community.

2.1.4 Coordination Systems

Communication is fundamental to any form of organizing, but it is pre-eminent in virtual organizations. Without communication, the boundary spanning among virtual entities would not be possible. Electronic communication enables parties to link across distance, time, culture, departments, and organizations, thereby creating *anyone/anytime/anyplace* alternatives to the traditional same-time, same-place, functionally-centered, in-house forms of organizational experience (O'Hara-Devereaux and Johansen, 1994).

		TIME		
		Same	**Different but predictable**	**Different and unpredictable**
PLACE	**Same**	Meeting facilitation	Work shifts	Team rooms
	Different but predictable	Teleconferencing Videoconferencing Desktop conferencing	Electronic mail	Collaborative writing
	Different and unpredictable	Interactive multicast seminars	Computer bboards	Workflow

Figure 2.3. Place and Time for Collaboration Systems (Source: Jonathan Grudin, "CSCW: History and Focus", Communications of the ACM, 37, 1, 92-105.)

Coordination systems address the problem of integration and harmonious adjustment of individuals' work efforts toward the accomplishment of a common goal. Examples of coordination systems include electronic calendars and automated meeting scheduling software. Coordination systems are liable to impose some rather heavy constraints on the people who use them. For example, in order for a system to automatically schedule a meeting it needs to know the private schedules of all people taking part in this meeting. Therefore, managers and executives mainly use these systems with personal secretaries who maintain their agendas. In contrast to other computer-supported cooperative work systems (groupware), in coordination systems communication plays a minor part; it is less important than the envisioned goal of the system. Coordination systems are generally used in an asynchronous and remote way.

The task and media fit on information richness

Increasing potential richness required for task success ↓	Media for Group Communication System — Increasing potential richness of information →			
Task types(s)	Computer systems	Audio systems	Video systems	Face-to-face communications
Generating ideas and plans	Good fit	Marginal fit Info too rich	Poor fit Info too rich	Poor fit Info too rich
Choosing correct answer: intellective tasks	Marginal fit Medium too constrained	Good fit	Good fit	Poor fit Info too rich
Choosing preferred answer: judgment tasks	Poor fit Medium too constrained	Good fit	Good fit	Marginal fit Info too rich
Negotiating conflicts of interests	Poor fit Medium too constrained	Poor fit Medium too constrained	Marginal fit Info too lean	Good fit

Figure 2.4 Relationships between task characteristics and media richness

2.1.5 Co-authoring and Argumentation Systems

Co-authoring systems aim to support the cooperation necessary between co-authors in document production. In general, these systems support asynchronous cooperation with each group member working independently on a specific portion of the document. Reviews and comments may be added to the document later by annotating sections of it (Rodden, 1991). Co-authoring systems are not distinguished by the location of their users, who can be either remote or co-located.

Argumentation systems support the structured development of multiparty arguments and negotiations. A well-known example is the gIBIS system which is described by Begeman and Conklin (1988). Due to the many and very diverse activities that may be distinguished within a co-authoring environment, argumentation systems are useful additions to co-authoring systems.

2.1.6 Electronic Mail and Messaging

Electronic messaging is clearly a widely used technology for providing effective notification. Messaging systems are based on the idea of 'pushing' information from source to destination (as opposed to bulletin boards, for example, where information is 'pulled' from source to destination).

Electronic messaging effectively relaxes constraints of time and place in situations where the communications are *one-to-one*. The success of e-mail in these situations has led to users stretching e-mail functionality further. For example, mailing lists and list servers are used for *one-to-many* communications and message stores are being used as persistent data stores to support *many-to-many* communications. Messaging systems are not however ideal for coping with the complex information management which *many-to-many* communication requires.

Electronic mail actually began as a messaging function of groupware. According to Tom Van Vleck at his website, "The History of Electronic Mail", the Compatible Time-Sharing System (CTSS) was begun at MIT in 1961. It allowed multiple users to log into the IBM 7094 from remote dial-up terminals, and to store files online on disk. To put it into context in comparison to today's computing, a standard IBM 7094 had 32K 36-bit words of memory. Its data channels could access memory and run simple channel programs to do I/O once started by the CPU, and the channels could cause a CPU interrupt when the I/O finished. They cost about $3.5 million back then (Van Vleck, 2001).

This new storing ability encouraged users to share information in new ways. When CTSS users wanted to pass messages to each other, they sometimes created files with names like "TO SAM" and put them in "common file" directories, e.g. M1416 CMFL03. The recipient could log into CTSS later, from any terminal, and look for the file, and print it out if it was there (Van Vleck, 2001).

The CTSS MAIL command was proposed in an undated Programming Staff Note 49 by people working on the design of a new, improved file system for CTSS with many additional features. Numerical sequence places the note in either December 64 or January 65. PSN 49 proposed a facility for the system operators so they could inform users when lost files were retrieved from tape, by sending a message to a file in their directory (Van Vleck, 2001).

The MAIL command created or appended to a file called MAIL BOX in the recipient's home directory. Privileged users could send URGENT MAIL instead, and could send mail even if the user's disk quota was exhausted. The LOGIN command was modified to print 'YOU HAVE MAIL BOX' or 'YOU HAVE URGENT MAIL' at login if these files existed and had nonzero length (Van Vleck, 2001).

According to Van Vleck (2001), this may now been seen as humorous that the MIT staff were nervous at the time about ticking off the US Post Office by calling the facility MAIL, which was thought by some to be a 'Bad Idea', because they feared the Post Office would require the destruction of a first class stamp for each message sent.

So messaging within a single-computer time-sharing system at a university or a large company such as IBM has been around since the early 1960s. However, e-mail between computers, as we currently recognize it, came into being in 1971 when Ray Tomlinson at Bolt Beranek and Newman became the first person to send a message from a computer on one network to a computer on another network (Kay, 2001).

Tomlinson is the undisputed source for the way we write e-mail addresses. Limited by a caps-only printing terminal, Tomlinson decided on the now-ubiquitous @ symbol to separate the user name from the computer name and to indicate that the address was outside the local network. "The @ sign seemed to make sense," Tomlinson later recalled. "I used the @ sign to indicate that the user was 'at' some other host, rather than being local." (Kay, 2001).

As e-mail has matured from being an internal notepad to a mission-critical technology, administering messaging systems has become one of the most complex tasks in the enterprise.

Messaging tasks include the creation, storage, exchange, and management of text, images, voice, telex, fax, e-mail, paging, and Electronic Data Interchange (EDI) over a communications network. A messaging server acts as a message exchange program for client programs.

There are two major messaging server models: the point-to-point model and the publish/subscribe model. In the point-to-point model, shown in Figure 2.5, the message passing the sending application/client establishes a named message queue in the broker/server and sends messages to this queue. The receiving client registers with the broker to receive messages posted to this queue. There is a one-to-one relationship between the sending and receiving clients.

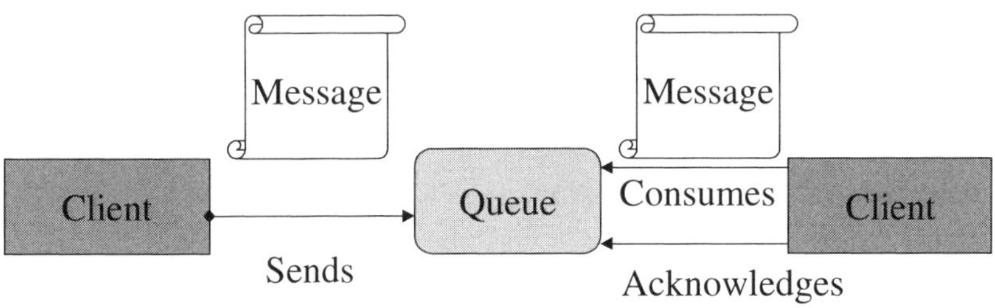

Figure 2.5 Point-to-point message serving model (Adapted from source: Sun Microsystems)

In a publish/subscribe (pub/sub) model (Figure 2.6), clients address messages to a topic. Publishers and subscribers are generally anonymous and may dynamically publish or subscribe to the content hierarchy. The system takes care of distributing the messages arriving from a topic's multiple publishers to its multiple subscribers. Topics retain messages only as long as it takes to distribute them to current subscribers (Sun Microsystems, 2003).

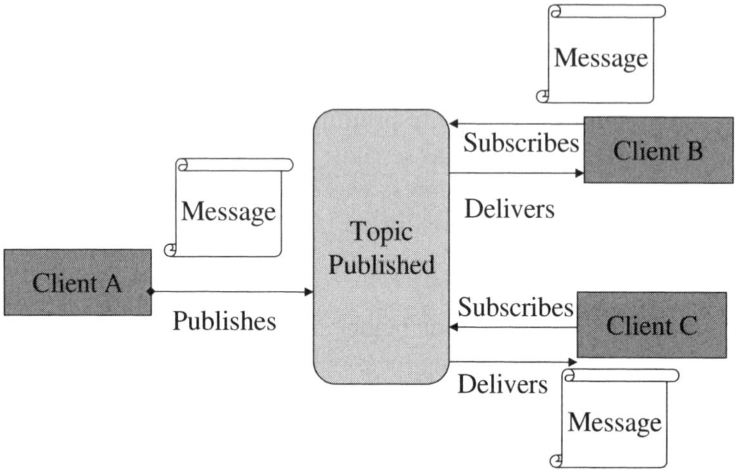

Figure 2.6 Pub/sub messaging model (Adapted from source: Sun Microsystems)

Pub/sub messaging has the following characteristics:

- Each message may have multiple consumers.
- Publishers and subscribers have a timing dependency. A client that subscribes to a topic can consume only messages published after the client has created a subscription, and the subscriber must continue to be active in order for it to consume messages.

Messaging allows programs to share common message-handling code, to isolate resources and interdependencies, and to easily handle an increase in message volume. Messaging also makes it easier for programs to communicate across different programming environments (languages, compilers, and operating systems) since the only thing that each environment needs to understand is the common messaging format and protocol (Sun Microsystems, 2003).

2.1.7 Calendaring and Scheduling (C&S)

In contrast to messaging systems (i.e., systems that push information), bulletin boards, computer conferencing systems, shared databases, web sites, etc., are technologies that mainly support 'information pull'. These systems avoid several of the limitations of messaging systems and leave more of the communication control in the hands of the recipients rather than the senders.

However, for some communication requirements, approaches that rely solely on 'information pull' have their own shortcomings associated with not actively notifying users.

Open Internet standards are necessary for calendaring and scheduling (C&S) applications to interoperate. Standards for C&S applications have yet to be defined, so current C&S applications are, by definition, proprietary. Each application, as shown in Figure 2.7, uses its own proprietary communication protocol, making it impossible for calendar applications to interoperate without gateways.

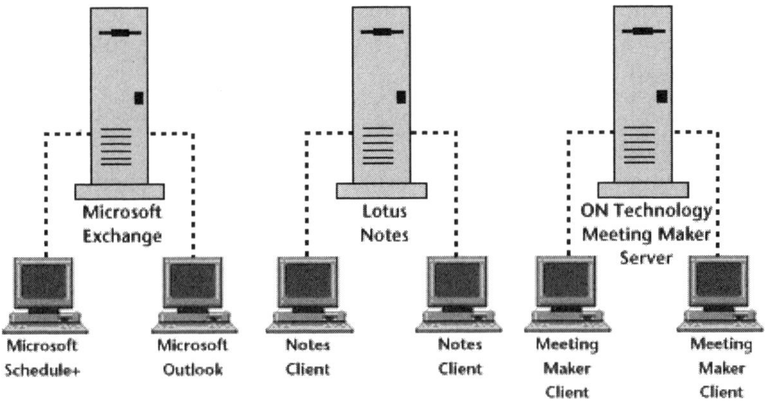

Figure 2.7 Calendar and scheduling infrastructure

The lack of C&S standards has resulted in the following interoperability problems:

Users cannot choose their own calendaring and scheduling application. Today users can't choose a personal C&S application and maintain interoperability with other users in an organization. For example, if an organization selects On Technology's Meeting Maker, all users in the company must use the Meeting Maker client. Anyone who prefers a different C&S application – for example, Starfish Software's Sidekick 97 or Lotus Organizer – is forced to use two different C&S clients. Typically, users must manually copy information from one application to another.

Users on one calendaring and scheduling system cannot communicate with users on another. Currently, separate organizations typically cannot schedule meetings with each other. For example, if an organization has one set of users with Microsoft Schedule+ and Exchange and another set with On Technology's Meeting Maker, the users have no convenient way of communicating with each other. They must go outside the C&S system and do their scheduling via e-mail or telephone. This is often true even if two organizations are using the same C&S solution. Because most C&S systems available today were designed for use behind a corporate firewall on a trusted network, they are not suitable for Internet calendaring and scheduling.

Users have not been able to easily exchange information between their electronic organizers and their organization's calendaring and scheduling system. Standards-based mechanisms for exchanging C&S information have not existed until very recently. The lack of standards has forced C&S vendors to write specific import and export utilities for each electronic organizer. As a result, many PC-based calendaring products do not interoperate well with other products or electronic organizers.

IETF Calendaring and Scheduling Working Group has been defining three standards:

- a calendaring data interchange format or core object specification based on vCalendar and called iCalendar
- a calendaring interoperability protocol
- a calendar access protocol.

Several major C&S vendors support vCard and vCalendar, including Netscape.

2.1.8 Conferencing

"This 'telephone' has too many shortcomings to be seriously considered as a means of communication. The device is inherently of no value to us." – Western Union internal memo, 1876.

Audio conferencing (also called 'teleconferencing') means communicating over a telephone line with three or more participants.

The capacity of audio conferencing systems can be hundreds of callers on a single conference call. While most business, education and government audio conferences take place with less than twenty callers, there are some unique applications that require far more capacity. For example, Wall Street conference calls to announce earnings, products and management changes are typically served by very high capacity systems with hundreds of callers listening in.

Features of audio conference systems vary widely; however, all offer more capability than typical office phone systems. For example, in a conference call of more than just a few callers, it is typical that one or more callers are hard to hear. Audio conferencing systems and service providers can usually adjust the audio volume, or gain, of any individual caller to more closely match the audio levels of other callers. This can make all the difference in success or failure of a teleconference call. Further, special features such as requests for an operator, breakout groups and custom billing are common.

Quality is a key factor in the success of teleconferencing. In fact, if audio quality is poor, the primary objective of the call can be lost. Nearly all modern audio conferencing systems have important capabilities including echo cancellation and automatic gain control that are not available on most telephone systems. Moreover, most commercial telephone systems are not engineered to link multiple callers. So, while it may seem that simply pushing the 'conference' button on several telephones to add additional callers will do the job, in fact the audio quality of teleconferences pieced together this way can be quite poor.

Video conferencing is interactive two-way visual and audio communication over a distance. It is often referred to as *videoconferencing* or *video teleconferencing*, as both terms are used in industry. It is one of many technologies within the domain of *video communications* including broadcast television, video streaming, video assessment and video collaboration.

Video conferencing first became commercially available in the 1970s as a unique form of communicating over great distances. However, prior to the mid-1980s the high cost of equipment, network lines and its comparably poor quality kept it out of mainstream business use. Then, in the early 1990s, digital communication service offerings such as ISDN and Switched Digital Service began to be offered, laying the foundational network capability that has enabled widespread use of video technologies including video conferencing.

Deployment of network technologies has been, and remains, key to widespread commercial adoption of video communications. Today, video conferencing equipment, software and services are widely available at prices that even small organizations can afford. Additionally, video communications transport networks can now take many forms – from plain old telephone service (POTS), to Integrated Services Digital Networks (ISDN) and even to Internet Protocol (IP) networks, common in most office environments.

Video conferencing systems vary widely; however, the features of most systems are expanding rapidly and the interoperation among products from leading manufacturers is excellent. For example, most video conferencing systems support two monitors and two cameras, one each for people and documents. While features are becoming plentiful, most modern video conference systems can be operated with a simple remote control – similar to those used to operate a consumer television.

Although today there are a number of superb video conferencing products on the market, each supporting a wide array of features, choosing the best product can be quite difficult. Technical considerations include choosing a network type, selecting equipment capabilities, finding a quality vendor and consideration of the video conference meeting room environment.

Group decision support systems

In 1984, Paul Cashman and Irene Grief organized a workshop of people from various disciplines who shared an interest in how people work, with an eye to understanding how technology could support them. They coined the term "computer-supported cooperative work" to describe this common interest (Grudin, 1994a). Over the past decade thousands of researchers and developers have been drawn to it. The first conferences were held in the United States, but the topic was picked up immediately in Europe and Asia, where related work and serious interest already existed. An earlier approach to group support, "Office Automation", had run out of steam. The problems were not primarily technical, although technical challenges certainly existed. The key problem was understanding system requirements. In the mid-1960s, tasks such as filling seats on airplane flights or printing payroll checks had been translated into requirements that resulted (with some trial and error) in successful mainframe systems. In the mid-1970s, minicomputers promised to support groups and organizations in more sophisticated, interactive ways: Office Automation was born. Single-user applications such as word processors and spreadsheets succeeded; office automation tried to integrate and extend these successes to support groups and departments (Grudin, 1994a).

Building technology was not enough for success. Designers needed to learn more about how people work in groups and organizations and how technology affects that. Some in the Management Information Systems field had promoted this as a way to improve success rates in large system development. But it had been largely absent from discourse among designers and developers in the vendor company settings engaged in early efforts to develop group support applications. CSCW started as an effort by technologists to learn from economists, social psychologists, anthropologists, organizational theorists, educators, and anyone else who could shed light on group activity.

CSCW has also become a place for system-builders to share experiences and inform others of technical possibilities and constraints. Applications include desktop conferencing and videoconferencing systems, collaborative authorship applications, electronic mail and its refinements and extensions, and electronic meeting rooms or group support systems. Other application domains that are related but not strongly represented include Computer-Assisted Design/Computer-Assisted Manufacturing (CAD/CAM), Computer-Assisted Software Engineering (CASE), concurrent engineering, workflow management, distance learning, telemedicine, and the real-time network conferences called MUDs (after 'multi-user dungeons', although they are now used for more than game-playing) (Grudin, 1994a).

The term CSCW has survived all these years, but has been criticized for violating the maxim that four words are too many (some use 'computer-supported collaboration' or CSC). Frankly, 'cooperative' work is often more a goal than a reality. 'Workgroup computing' shifts the focus from the work being supported to the technology and restricts it to small organizational units. So does 'groupware', used by Peter and Trudy Johnson-Lenz prior to 1984 and adopted by the CSCW community (Grudin, 1994a).

As off-the-shelf single-user product developers extended their view to computer support for groups, many confronted issues in group dynamics for the first time. The design of applications such as word processors stressed perceptual and cognitive factors. Developers often succeeded with minimal attention to the actual workplaces in which single-user applications were used. With groupware, social, motivational, and political aspects of workplaces suddenly become crucial (Grudin, 1994b). And as large systems declined in cost, smaller organizational units used them. GDSS, once expensive and marketed for use in high-level decision-making, have evolved into 'group support systems,' less expensive and flexible enough to support a variety of meeting types.

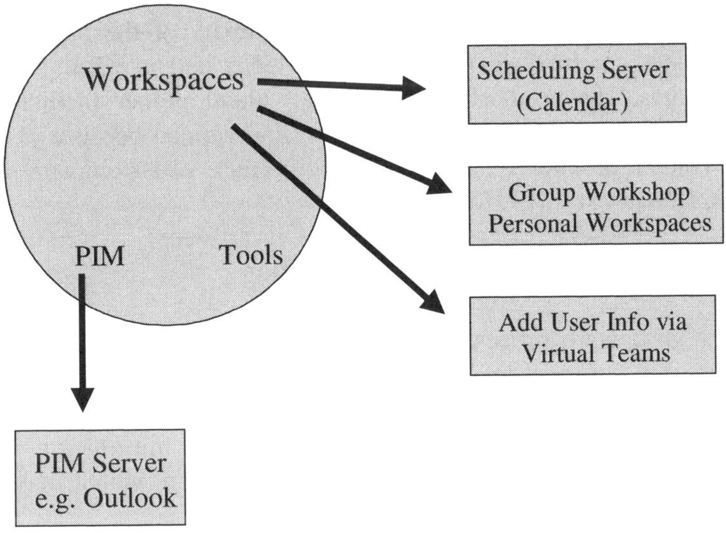

Figure 2.8 Workflow Systems

Figure 2.8 shows the evolution of workflow systems. Group Support Systems (GSS) are software tools, each of which uniquely focuses on enhancing specific team dynamics or processes (Nunamaker, Dennis *et al.*, 1991). Through structured techniques, GSS facilitates rapid discussion of opinions in a minimum amount of time (Dennis, Nunamaker *et al.*, 1991). Examples of specific GSS tools include brainstorming, idea generation (Robichaux and Cooper 1998), open discussion, idea organization, issue analysis, alternative analysis, questionnaires, polling, group writing, and process modeling (Nunamaker, Dennis *et al.*, 1991).

GSS not only includes software but also includes two other components: (1) the GSS-trained facilitator, who sets ground rules, enforces protocols, maintains group memory, selects appropriate software tools, maintains the agenda, and champions the use of GSS (Nunamaker, Briggs *et al.*, 1997). (2) the GSS meeting room and facilities (Dean, Lee *et al.*, 1995). This triumvirate of GSS components works together to provide a potential synergy not found in ordinary groupware or typical group meetings. Given the potential benefits of GSS, it is not surprising to find more satisfaction in group problem-solving in GSS groups as compared to non-GSS groups (Gallupe, Dennis *et al.*, 1992). The resulting decisions of GSS teams have higher buy-in than in non-GSS teams (Nunamaker, Briggs *et al.*, 1997).

GSS is not always a positive outcome in groupwork. For example, GSS does not overcome poor leadership (Nunamaker, Briggs *et al.*, 1997); therefore, GSS could make a bad leadership situation worse. Parallel communication can easily produce too much information too fast (Dennis, Hayes *et al.*, 1999). Depending on the complexity of the problem being solved, issues can arise in regard to consistency and integration of group ideas (Dennis, Hayes *et al.*, 1999). And without proper facilitation, the performance of established groups may be undermined because of "Group Think" (Mennecke and Valacich 1998) or because of a dominant majority (Dennis, Hilmer *et al.*, 1997).

2.1.9 Principles: Factors in Decision Making

Different groupware processes have different effects on attention to and integration of information, and ultimately decision quality. Groupware processes that provide categories to organize information and those that require the receiver of information to categorize information improve attention to information and integration of information, which may lead to improved decision quality.

Table 2.1 General Benefits of GSS (Lowry and Wilson, 2000)

Anonymity	provides anonymity which increases the volume and quality of ideas (Gallupe, Dennis *et al.*, 1992); promotes open exploration and criticism without fear of reprisals (Diehl and Stroebe 1987) or the influence of politics (Nunamaker, Briggs *et al.*, 1997); changes criticism into a signal to suggest other ideas and provides more objectivity (Nunamaker, Briggs *et al.*, 1997).
Communication	helps remove communication barriers (DeSanctis and Gallupe 1987).
Efficiency	promotes efficiency, allowing more expert involvement (Dennis, Hayes *et al.*, 1999).
Apprehension	helps overcome evaluation apprehension (Gallupe, Dennis *et al.*, 1992).
Group Size	allows larger groups to effectively participate in meetings than could traditionally take place (Nunamaker, Dennis *et al.*, 1991).
Learning	supports organizational learning and memory (Nunamaker, Dennis *et al.*, 1991).
Parallel Communication	allows all group members to simultaneously enter information, providing an equal opportunity for participation (Nunamaker, Dennis *et al.*, 1991).
Positive Behavior	discourages behavior, such as domination, that can negatively impact meeting productivity (Nunamaker, Dennis *et al.*, 1991).
Process Support Flexibility	supports three types of processes according to the group's needs: (1) chauffeured, where one person facilitates and uses the GSS, and walks participants through the process (Nunamaker, Dennis *et al.*, 1991), (2) supported, where participants have their own GSS workstations to provide anonymous, parallel feedback (Nunamaker, Dennis *et al.*, 1991), (3) interactive, which adds to the supported process by adding a strong group memory (Nunamaker, Dennis *et al.*, 1991).
Production Blocking	helps overcome production blocking (Gallupe, Bastianutti *et al.*, 1991).
Quality	teams produce higher quality results (Gallupe, Dennis *et al.*, 1992).
Task Flexibility	allows groups to choose from many structured or unstructured techniques and methods to perform their meeting task (Nunamaker, Dennis *et al.*, 1991).
Task Structure	Task structure (DeSanctis and Gallupe 1987) helps a group analyze task-related information, which helps users make better decisions (Nunamaker, Dennis *et al.*, 1991).
Task Support	provides task support (Dennis, George *et al.*, 1988), which helps improve analysis by providing better information and synergy in the use of the information by the group (Nunamaker, Dennis *et al.*, 1991).

There are several factors determining decision structure that can be aided by groupware:

- The importance of the quality of the decision
- The extent to which the decision makers possesses the knowledge and expertise to make the decision
- The extent to which potential participants have the necessary information
- The degree of structuredness of the problem context
- The degree to which acceptance or commitment is critical to successful implementation
- The probability of acceptance
- The degree of motivation among the participants to achieve organizational goals
- The degree of potential conflict among the participants.

2.1.10 Multiparticipant Decision-Maker (MDM) Rationale

Why work with a multiparticipant decision-maker (MDM) system, such as CSCW, groupware or other forms of collaborative work? What benefits or drawbacks are involved in decision-making with others? The following list outlines both the sources of gains and the potential for losses in using MDM, versus a single decision-maker.

Sources of Gains in MDM Activities

- Collective has greater knowledge than any single participant
- Allows for synergistic results otherwise not obtainable
- Interaction stimulates the generation of knowledge or information otherwise unavailable
- Participants can improve individual performance through learning from others
- Improved evaluation over individual decision-making structure.

Sources of Losses in MDM Activities

- Relative allocation of speaking time is reduced with MDM size
- Can result in idea production blocking
- Can produce information overload much faster
- Participants may not be able to remember all the contributions of others
- Pressures resulting in conformity can be exacerbated
- Can increase evaluation apprehension in participants
- Allows for ‘free-riding’ or social loafing of lazy or non-participative individuals
- Can promote cognitive inertia or groupthink
- Increases opportunity for socialization over goal focus

- Increases decision context coordination activities
- Can allow for partial task or knowledge analysis.

2.1.11 Motivation and Methods

Adaptability is a critical criterion in determining the potential success of a groupware application. Applications that allow users to adapt the technologies to their own needs and uses allow social behaviors to rule interactions as appropriate and provide the opportunity for co-development of the technology and the work activity. In particular, it means not building a set of procedures and structures into the technology that dictate group behavior. Groupware in this case may be appropriate when:

- There is a need for consensus
- Expertise is distributed among individuals
- Organizational commitment to decision is desired.

The last point may be key to getting the right numbers to use the groupware. Critical mass means having enough users; furthermore these must be people the user wants to talk to, and collaborate with. The importance of critical mass can be illustrated by a number of examples of both asynchronous and synchronous groupware: a Lotus Notes discussion database can fail as a forum for exchanging ideas because there is an insufficiently large number of contributors, so that discussions and topics rapidly become stale. Research prototypes in collaboration technologies have also suffered from lack of critical mass: there is little benefit to having desktop videoconferencing, or lightweight electronic paging technology, if your recipient lacks the hardware and software to communicate using these.

Since critical mass may not occur in the short term, there are several commercial alternatives for outsourced groupware coordination, based on a price per participant:

- Covision's Council (www.covision.com) is a groupware application and service, running on a network of laptop computers, and provides audience polling, brainstorming and decision making applications. Council's tools fall into three categories: text gathering, polling and recording. Council has been used with as many as 1500 people, on portable networks of up to 200 laptop computers, but groups of 20 are more common.
- Enterprise Solutions' Meetingworks (www.meetingworks.com) is a local area network application-based group decision support system with additional Web-based modules.
- GroupSystems' (formerly Ventana Corporation) Workgroup Edition 2.0 (www.groupsystems.com) provides services for automating collaborative

decision-making. Their current LAN-based product is migrating to a browser-based system.

In an interactive group, the critical mass of methods of working are just as important as the necessary technological processes behind the interaction solution. It is not a 'free for all': there are methods for brainstorming activities, and ways to create a list of alternatives and have a discussion on the alternatives.

To examine this, we will use the classification scheme that was defined by DeSanctis and Gallupe (1987), where "level 1" systems provide technical features, "level 2" systems add modeling and group decision techniques, and "level 3" systems extend this support with machine-induced decision aids and recommendations.

Table 2.2 DeSantis and Gallupe MDM System Classification

MDM Level	*Participant Needs*	*System Feature*
1 Reduce Communication Barriers	Message passing among participants Access to data files during meeting Simultaneous display of ideas, graphs, votes, etc. To all participants Relaxation of inhibitions to contribute Control for free-riders Organization and analysis of ideas and votes Preference quantification Agenda planning Schedule coordination	Electronic messaging Computer networking Large shared viewing screen or public display window Anonymous contribution Active solicitation of ideas Summarization and tabulation Rating/ranking scales Agenda templates Continuous display of progress
2 Reduce Uncertainty and Noise	Problem structuring and solution scheduling Uncertainty analysis Analysis of resource allocation problems Data analysis Preference analysis Structured guidance of deliberations	Automated planning methods (PERT, etc.) Decision tables, trees, etc. LP and optimization modeling Statistical tools Subjective probability methods MDM coordination methods (nominal, etc.)
3 Regulate Decision Processes	Enforcement of formal decision procedures Increased clarity of options for decision procedures Structuring and filtering of messages to adhere to rules Development of deliberation governance rules	Automated procedure mechanisms Automated advisor for providing advice regarding various approaches Structuring and filter agents Rule set construction and inference mechanisms

There are several styles of functional facilities associated with groupwork. Kraemer and King (1988) distinguishes between six *technological systems*:

- Electronic Boardroom – conference room with computer-controlled audiovisual wide-screen projection capabilities. Multiparticipants need to be at the same time/same place. *Application needed to retrieve presentation.*
- Teleconference Room – conference room with computer-controlled audiovisual transmission between locations. Multiparticipants are at the same time in different places. *Application to control digital transmission of audio, voice and data.*
- Group Network – separate office facilities connected via a computer network. Same or different time/different places. *Application for conferencing and exchange of video, audio and data*
- Information Center – conference room with video projector for windscreen viewing. Individual computers with display terminals. Same time/same place interaction. Applications software are needed. *Applications needed word processor, data management, statistical analysis, graphics.*
- Collaboration Laboratory – conference room with electronic whiteboard and networked computers. *Application for collaborative interaction and information exchange*
- Decision Room – conference room with video projector for widescreen viewing and networked computers. *Application to support decision analysis, brainstorming, modeling, etc.*

Technology rationale for support of these kinds of multiparticipant decision-making (MDM) systems is dependent on a number of variables:
- Local and wide-area telecommunications
- Quick transfer of large amount of data
- Establishment of networking and operating system standards
- Multi-platform support
- Improvement in hardware and software support
- Improvement in value-to-cost ratio.

It has been found that it is best to use technology to enhance group activities if any of the following apply:
- Anonymity important: sensitive issues need to be discussed which participants might be reluctant to discuss openly
- There is an extreme (even violent) difference of opinions among dominant personalities

- Consensus is needed before going forward
- Multiple perspectives/expertise are necessary to make a good decision
- There is a limited time to collect information from a large group of people
- A very complex decision, based on multiple criteria, must be made
- The meeting content must be quickly documented and used for desired impact on the organization.

Privacy and anonymity can be important issues in collaboration. For example, personal calendars in groupware spaces may contain a range of information, such as: meeting titles; conference room numbers and other location information (restaurant names, for example); names of co-workers, friends, family, external business contacts; phone numbers; and task information. Privacy also encompasses issues of *company security* of information. Employees in certain job positions might be especially sensitive to this concern, and may keep their calendars restricted or closed for this reason, despite seeing the benefit of open calendars otherwise. Management, especially executive management, are among those who may have company-sensitive information in these calendars.

Do not use technology with anonymity for these types of group activities:

- One-way communication; dissemination of information (consider using e-mail, memos, or videos); working sessions in which individuals need to work independently with some type of personal productivity tool such as a word processor or spreadsheet (an exception might be sub-group breakout sessions in which small groups work in teams on specific sections of a document or project that is shared by the entire group).
- Sharing the blame (also known as "getting everyone in the boat with you"). When decisions have really already been made and the boss wants to garner the group's approval, an anonymous environment is the last thing he or she needs; all kinds of resistance will surface under the cover of anonymity.
- Gatherings designed to showcase an individual's abilities.

Distributed systems have grown from company-wide networks to include global federations of independent and separately managed systems, such as the Internet. The dynamism of global computing systems means that computational entities which offer services will be confronted with requests from entities that they have never met before; mobile entities will need to obtain services within environments that are unfamiliar and possibly hostile. A party faced with such a complex world stands to benefit, but only if it can respond to new entities and assign meaningful privileges to them. Examples of collaboration systems in use include:

- ForComment (Access Technologies): Helps a group of writers and reviewers agree on the content of a document
- Instant Update (ON Technologies): Allows several user to write a document jointly
- Lotus Notes (Lotus Development): Allows information distribution and scheduling.

Social and technical factors interact to create patterns of technology use, and technology use is best understood in light of its social context. *Task Fit* as a factor influencing group use of technology refers to the degree to which the technology assists individuals and the whole group in accomplishing its work. *Process Fit* as a factor influencing group use of technology involves the degree to which technology matches the work practices and culture of the group. Therefore, rationale and triggers for adoption of collaborative solutions need to address both the task and process fit of the activity.

Rationale and triggers for adoption include:

- Multipurpose and flexible
- Encourages user involvement
- Not only user-friendly but also user-seductive
- Provides different levels of anonymity
- Reduces group pathologies
- Increases effectiveness, efficiency and satisfaction of decision making process.

2.2 Groupware Applications and Intranets

Groupware offers significant advantages over single-user systems. These are some of the more common reasons people want to use groupware:

- to facilitate communication: make it faster, clearer, more persuasive
- to enable communication where it wouldn't otherwise be possible
- to enable telecommuting
- to cut down on travel costs
- to bring together multiple perspectives and expertise
- to save time and cost in coordinating group work.

In the business world, Groupware applications can significantly improve the customer service experience, by allowing individuals within an organization to quickly notify other members (i.e., managers, supervisors, etc.) of customer problems without ever leaving their desk. Groupware applications can also help service-oriented businesses schedule jobs without overlapping appointments or overloading one employee with too many service calls.

Some other examples of groupware applications at work could be the ability to assign tasks to employee (e.g., call a customer, finish a project, deliver documents, etc.) that must be accomplished within a specific period of time. This facilitates a more accurate method of communication that cannot be questioned later when tasks are not completed properly.

There are typically several types of common groupware applications with their own associated design options. Comparing those design options across applications yields interesting new perspectives on well-known applications. Also, in many cases, these systems can be used together, and, in fact, are intended to be used in conjunction. For example, group calendars are used to schedule videoconferencing meetings, multi-player games use live video and chat to communicate, and newsgroup discussions spawn more highly-involved interactions among large groups of people.

2.2.1 Asynchronous Groupware – Definitions

E-mail is by far the most common groupware application (besides of course, the traditional telephone). While the basic technology is designed to pass simple messages between two people, even relatively basic e-mail systems today typically include interesting features for forwarding messages, filing messages, creating mailing groups, and attaching files with a message. Other features that have been explored include: automatic sorting and processing of messages, automatic routing, and structured communication (messages requiring certain information).

Newsgroups and mailing lists are similar in spirit to e-mail systems except that they are intended for messages among large groups of people instead of 1-to-1 communication. In practice the main difference between newsgroups and mailing lists is that newsgroups only show messages to a user when they are explicitly requested (an 'on-demand' service), while mailing lists deliver messages as they become available (an 'interrupt-driven' interface).

Workflow systems allow documents to be routed through organizations through a relatively fixed process. A simple example of a workflow application is an expense report in an organization: an employee enters an expense report and submits it, a copy is archived then routed to the employee's manager for approval, the manager receives the document, electronically approves it and sends it on, and the expense is registered to the group's account and forwarded to the accounting department for payment. Workflow systems may provide features such as routing, development of forms, and support for differing roles and privileges.

Hypertext is a system for linking text documents to each other, with the Web being an obvious example. Whenever multiple people author and link documents, the system becomes group work, constantly evolving and responding to others' work. Some hypertext systems include capabilities for seeing who else has visited a certain page or link, or at least seeing how often a link has been followed, thus giving users a basic awareness of what other people are doing in the system. Page counters on the Web are a crude approximation of this function. Another common multi-user feature in hypertext (that is not found on the Web) is allowing any user to create links from any page, so that others can be informed when there are relevant links that the original author was unaware of.

Group calendars allow scheduling, project management, and coordination among many people, and may provide support for scheduling service calls as well. Typical features detect when schedules conflict or find meeting times that will work for everyone. Group calendars also help to locate people. Typical concerns are privacy (users may feel that certain activities are not public matters), completeness and accuracy (users may feel that the time it takes to enter schedule information is not justified by the benefits of the calendar).

Collaborative writing systems may provide both real time support and non-real time support. Word processors may provide asynchronous support by showing authorship and by allowing users to track changes and make annotations to documents. Authors collaborating on a document may also be given tools to help plan and coordinate the authoring process, such as methods for locking parts of the document or linking separately-authored documents. Synchronous support allows authors to see each other's changes as they make them, and usually needs to provide an additional communication channel to the authors as they work (via videophones or chat).

2.2.2 Synchronous or Real Time Groupware – Definitions

Shared whiteboards allow two or more people to view and draw on a shared drawing surface even from different locations. This can be used, for instance, during a phone call, where each person can jot down notes (e.g., a name, phone number, or map) or to work collaboratively on a visual problem. Most shared whiteboards are designed for informal conversation, but they may also serve structured communications or more sophisticated drawing tasks, such as collaborative graphic design, publishing, or engineering applications. Shared whiteboards can indicate where each person is drawing or pointing by showing telepointers, which are color-coded or labeled to identify each person.

Video communications systems allow two-way or multi-way calling with live video, essentially a telephone system with an additional visual component. Cost and compatibility issues limited early use of video systems to scheduled videoconference meeting rooms. Video is advantageous when visual information is being discussed, but may not provide substantial benefit in most cases where conventional audio telephones are adequate. In addition to supporting conversations, video may also be used in less direct collaborative situations, such as by providing a view of activities at a remote location.

Chat systems permit many people to write messages in real time in a public space. As each person submits a message, it appears at the bottom of a scrolling screen. Chat groups are usually formed by having chat rooms listed by name, location, number of people, topic of discussion, etc.

Many systems allow for rooms with controlled access or with moderators to lead the discussions, but most of the topics of interest to researchers involve issues related to unmoderated real-time communication including: anonymity, following the stream of conversation, scalability with number of users, and abusive users.

While chat-like systems are possible using non-text media, the text version of chat has the rather interesting aspect of having a direct transcript of the conversation. This not only has long-term value, but also allows for backward reference during conversation making it easier for people to drop into a conversation and still pick up on the ongoing discussion.

Decision support systems are designed to facilitate groups in decision-making. They provide tools for brainstorming, critiquing ideas, putting weights and probabilities on events and alternatives, and voting. Such systems enable presumably more rational and even-handed decisions. Primarily designed to facilitate meetings, they encourage equal participation by, for instance, providing anonymity or enforcing turn-taking.

2.2.3 Ideal Groupware

Within most discussions of groupware there is a consensus that ideal groupware would provide full integration of the separately identified components *communication*, *collaboration*, and *coordination.* The idea that groupware provides integrated support for communication, collaboration, and coordination is now widely accepted. Figure 2.9, initially provided by

Lotus Corporation (now part of IBM), is a widely used diagram to convey the relationships between communication, collaboration, and coordination.

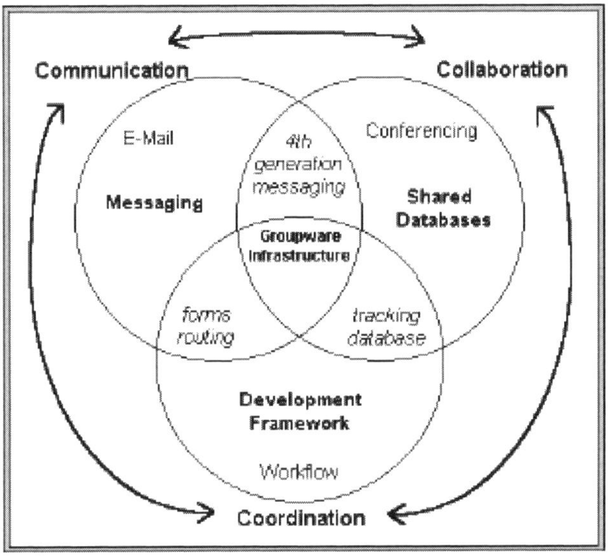

Figure 2.9 A view of groupware – based on diagrams from Lotus (1996)

Ideally, technologies should offer effective integration of techniques for both 'pushing' and 'pulling' information as required. Such technologies are emerging rapidly; they include web servers that automatically broadcast to subscribers (and contentiously clog up the networks in the process) as well as less contentious examples such as fourth-generation messaging systems that can embed live hyperlinks (to shared databases) within e-mail messages.

From the perspective of a technologist, the ideal enterprise-wide groupware would offer similarities to the diagram in terms of (Ginsburg and Duilba, 1997):

- Efficient protocols
- Portable, high-performance implementation
- Effective client interface (GUI) design
- Scalability
- Distributed management
- Interoperability with legacy systems
- Distributed Security.

The rationale for this list is that most real work involves dynamic movement between structured, unstructured, ad hoc, and pre-defined work, requiring an integrated push/pull model to support users as they move from one type of work to the next in the normal course of a process (Siviter *et al.*, 1997).

Structured, pre-defined group activities can be supported by programmatic workflow applications, of which there are two basic types: routing, based on messaging technology, and tracking, based on shared database technology. The integration of these two approaches to workflow automation is achieved through an integrated application development framework which exploits services of both messaging and shared database systems (Siviter *et al.*, 1997).

2.2.4 Groupware vs. Intranet

Groupware is software that helps groups of people communicate electronically. It is computer-mediated collaboration that increases the productivity or functionality of person-to-person processes (Coleman, 1992), and supports any time, any place (Johansen, 1991). Intranet allows the ability to use the Internet WWW technology within the 'intraprise' rather than for external connection to the Internet. Many collaborative functions are moving to the WWW and use the Internet as the input and output while still using traditional groupware on the LAN.

Groupware usually requires client software and that may mean costly licenses. Using internet technology means that only a browser is required for client usage. These either come with your operating system or can be obtained for free. Also, groupware in most cases requires you to use a particular brand and therefore entails a certain amount of 'lock-in' with your software supplier for future development. The use of client browsers with a standard desktop interface offers the easy integration with other applications, such as e-mail, faxes, scheduling, videoconferencing and active links within the body of a message.

2.2.5 Collaboration via Intranets

Another approach to collaboration activities through the Web is the creation of an intranet. An intranet is basically a platform based on internet principles accessible only to members of an organization/community. Technically, this is primarily based on the following protocols: HTTP (hypertext transmission protocol) at the server end, TCP/IP (transport control protocol/internet protocol) for network communication, and HTML (hypertext markup language protocol) at the browser end. While the Internet is an open-access platform, an intranet, however, is restricted to members of a community/organization through multi-layered security controls.

The key feature of this platform is its self-governance through horizontal connectivity. True, there are two classes of endpoints. There are servers that provide the information and surfers who browse and access information through the network. But, ideally speaking, they stand on the same pedestal in the sense that even the browsing machines can at the same time work as servers. This means that every receiver of information can also be a provider of information.

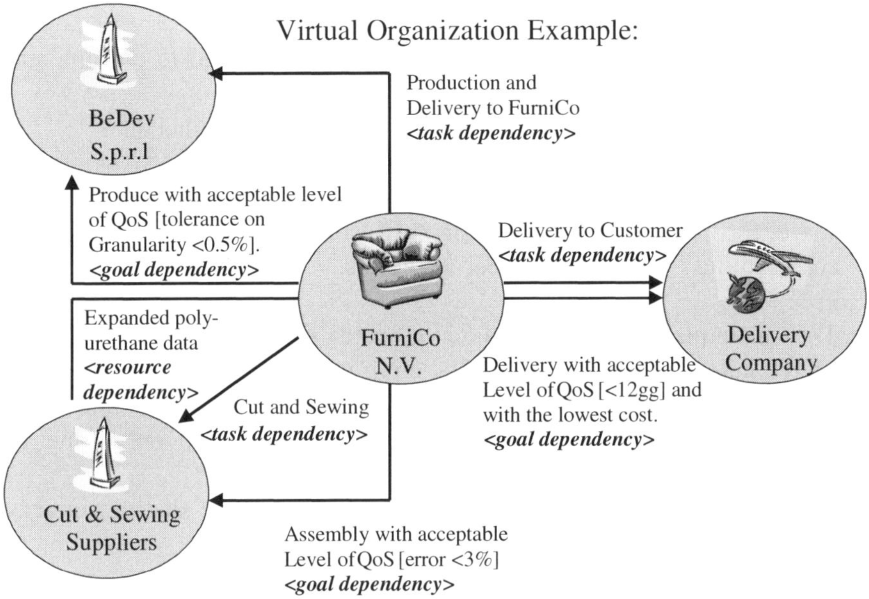

Figure 2.10 Example of collaboration via an Intranet

Members of the whole browsing community are potentially all linked with one-another, and can form into virtual groups depending on their interest through voluntary effort and without any centralized control (except perhaps for the limited function of maintaining the security gateway).

Intranet also provides a DRN (distributed resource network), where human resources separated across time and space can work together on a common project to leap-frog years of work in days. We have seen such efforts e.g. by teams who cracked the 64-bit security codes.

The intranet can provide the platform for a safe and secured information management system within the organization, helping people to collaborate as virtual teams, crossing boundaries of geography and time, as shown in Figure 2.10 above.

Typical information that can go into an intranet could include:

- human resource database – who is where, knows what, does what, has what interests

- recent news from departments/units – both organizational and personal (of interest to others in the organization), company announcements
- exchange of opinions on key issues affecting the organization
- repository of strategy papers, key manuals and working documents for easy access
- indexed repository of working papers, RFCs (request for comments – interestingly, the Internet standards are set and adhered to through such papers)
- utilities e.g. holiday lists, multi-layered access on personnel data
- exchange of ideas by working groups, task forces, people working on a particular project
- space for people to create their own columns for horizontal virtual communities – regulated by peer-set norms.

The same platform, extended to an outer ring (e.g. dealer networks, registered customers, online members, etc.), with limited accessibility, is an extranet. The extranet can be a meaningful platform for knowledge generation and sharing, in building relationships, and in enhancing the quality and effectiveness of service/support.

Intranets can cut transaction costs, help in knowledge sharing, increase access to information, and improve productivity and quality.

The key to a successful corporate intranet lies in its self-governance, the space and motivation available to people to participate and contribute. It is one thing to put together the most attractive, technologically savvy intranet platform, but a much tougher business is to ensure staff participation in accessing, using and putting up information.

Intranet architecture, therefore, is not a purely technological road map. It is all about how people are going to be interlinked. And this needs to be put together through a participatory process, learning by doing, learning from errors, learning through a culture of sharing and trust.

This is a small sample of the types of applications that can be in an intranet.

- Document Access
- Product Information
- Policies and Procedures
- Phone Directory
- Newsletters
- Project Information
- Official Travel Guide
- Employee Infobases
- Catalogs
- Newswire Clippings

- Software Libraries
- Art Libraries.

2.2.6 Enterprise Network Environment

The enterprise network environment is a critical factor in choosing a groupware system:

- often quite *heterogeneous* within the firm (fast LANs, employing 100 MB FDDI, or slower ones, employing 10 MB Ethernet); provisioning for slower dial-up access, e.g. 28.8K, or 64K ISDN.
- another layer of complexity: *multiplicity of connection protocols:* IBM SNA (System Network Architecture), TCP-IP, SPX/IPX, and NetBIOS.

The harder it is to get the network to communicate cohesively within the firm, the harder it will be to implement Notes and/or Web-based groupware solutions. Data networks form the backbone of any business, whether it is a distributed or centralized computing environment. The network empowers the enterprise by integrating business functions and enabling effective communication among various processes. Proper planning, dedicated implementation, post-integration support and training form a significant part of network management. The biggest challenge is to keep the existing network highly available or minimize the impact on the existing networking environment. Every growing organization faces the problem of congestion as increasing traffic results in clogging of network pathways.

A list of the features of an ideal enterprise-wide groupware system will naturally vary from firm to firm. However, a core set of features in major vendor offerings includes the following: unstructured information management, transaction security when updating shared resources, electronic mail and messaging, scheduling, group decision support systems, and workflow. Ideally, video and audio conferencing can be included in this list, but in practice corporate bandwidth is usually a constraining factor (Ginsburg and Duilba, 1997).

In practice, most attention is usually paid to the quality of electronic mail and workflow services. Document revision control is quite important, as is a robust store-and-forward electronic mail system that can reliably deliver large attachments; e.g. Word, Portable Document Format (PDF), or image (GIF or JPEG) files. Workflow and project management considerations require that simple electronic mail be enhanced with routing slips, automated acknowledgment-on-read tags, and encryption options (Ginsburg and Duilba, 1997).

2.2.7 Application Gateways

An application gateway is a firewall system in which service is provided by processes that maintain complete TCP connection state and sequencing. Application gateway firewalls often re-address traffic so that outgoing traffic appears to have originated from the firewall, rather than the internal host (Trusted Information System, 1998).

An application gateway is considered by experts to be the most secure type of firewall. All connections to the internal network go through the firewall. An application level firewall is distinguished by the use of security proxies (application gateways) for services such as FTP, TELNET, etc., which prevent direct access to services on the internal network.

The advantages of application gateways are that they:

- Do not allow any direct connections between internal and external hosts
- Support user-level authentication
- Analyze application commands inside the payload portion of data packets (whereas the stateful packet filters systems do not)
- Are able to keep comprehensive logs of traffic and specific activities.

The primary advantage of application gateway firewalls is that no direct connections are allowed through the firewall under any circumstances (Trusted Information System, 1998). Application gateway software is also referred to as proxy software, because the application gateway software running on the firewall 'stands in the gap' and looks like server software to the client, and client software to server.

The disadvantages of some application gateways are that they:

- Are slower than packet filters
- Require the internal client to know about them
- Do not support every possible type of connection.

One of the most onerous drawbacks of the initial generation of application gateways was that each workstation behind the firewall had to be configured to be aware of the firewall and had to have client software that is designed to be capable of communicating with the proxy software on the firewall. The introduction of transparency in application gateways means that in modern secure environments the client workstations do not either have to be aware of the firewall or run special software to communicate with the external network (Trusted Information System, 1998).

2.2.8 Information Repositories

Having an information repository provides a trusted information base, leveraging existing information whenever possible. Eventually most people need access to 'corporate data'. By having archives, companies have a collection of shared information used by the enterprise. The source of this archive depends on where information resides. To have the necessary archive tools, the enterprise may need to support extensions, different security levels, multiple feeds, filtering and daily updates. This could be a significant project.

A Web information repository provides cost savings, as it allows:

- Reduced cost of information sourcing
- Improved information quality
- Improved ability to manage information.

One expensive item is the trust of users, as it is critical to the success of an information repository. Therefore, a key cost is the cost of development, testing and production costs to reassure users of viability of the system.

In creating an information repository that is Web based, things to plan for in terms of viability also include:

- Ease of installation
- Functionality
- Integration into existing system services
- Knowing what you already know and have
- Scalability
- Third party tools.

2.2.9 Starting an intranet

Intranets and groupware can help employees communicate more effectively, capture and share their knowledge, and learn and innovate. Some of the first organizations to create internal Webs included Lockheed, Hughes and SAS Institute. Factors leading to the necessity of intranets include worldwide acceleration of user expectations due to globalization and spread of the Internet, and increasing needs for improving internal communication and knowledge worker productivity. Intranets can be fast, easy and cheap to implement, scalable, and flexible; they can capture and share expertise, create new business opportunities, and help leverage extranets for purposes like EDI.

Possible disadvantages of intranets include the potential for chaos, security risks, management fears, business culture clash, information overload, wasted productivity, and hidden or unknown costs.

Intranets have already been successfully deployed in numerous companies. EDS has acquired the right to place the U.S. Patent Information Services database on its intranet; it also provides its employees with a customized news report service called infoAlert via PointCast, and uses chat as part of its Global Communicators Network and IRC for a CIO weekly chat. Bell Atlantic's intranet saves several hundred thousand dollars through consolidation and reduced printing. Silicon Graphics has reported savings in processing requisitions via its intranet, Silicon Junction.

J.C. Penney's intranet, jWeb, helps cut costs in communicating between its offices in 37 countries. AT&T uses its intranet as a virtual meeting place (Hills, 1997). Booz Allen says its intranet has helped leverage its intellectual capital by recording its expertise and providing contact information for its consultants. Some such case studies are also available online, as in "How Sun Saves Money, Improves Service Using Internet Technologies." (Available at <http://www.sun.com/960101/feature1/>).

Some companies even obtain additional revenues on intranet sites by letting vendors advertise to their employees.

Groupware products help create an organizational memory, and boost communication, coordination and collaboration. These include functions like calendaring, scheduling, voice conferencing, videoconferencing, electronic meeting systems, data whiteboards, discussion and live chat. Due to the impact of the intranet, costs of groupware are coming down, and they are becoming increasingly Web-enabled.

According to Peter Sange, author of "The Fifth Discipline: The Art and Practice of the Learning Organization," the only sustainable competitive advantage comes from an organization's ability to learn. This will require the use of trained personnel as 'social systems analysts', according to Tom Davenport (1996), author of "Process Innovation: Reengineering Work Through Information Technology" (in his piece called "Software as Socialware", published in *CIO* magazine).

2.2.10 Intranet Reference Model

We need to think about providing tools to help people find information at multiple levels: on web pages, on local servers, and across the enterprise (and possibly at other intermediate levels as well).

In addition to the tools we will need to develop policies on what information can be searched (or found), and by what tools.

Finally, we are seeing the increasing need for people (yes, people) to be active participants in the discovery process. We call these people 'information finders' and their role is to identify the best-in-class information for use by other people. Librarians or functional experts play this role in some organizations today.

2.2.11 Information Mapping

Information Mapping is a method of bringing together current learning research and instructional technology into comprehensive materials development and presentation technology to improve technical communication. It can be seen as a system of principles and procedures for identifying, categorizing, interrelating and sequencing, as well as presenting graphically information required for learning and reference.

Information Mapping is a good methodology for presenting written information. It uses tactics such as white space, headings, summaries, layout and procedural techniques to present information in an easy-to-scan form. It is ideal for complex material and greatly assists with minimizing the time a user must spend on their information quest.

It is, however, not simply a layout technique. It is a technique that assists in determining the sequence of information, the quantity of information, the level of detail, the steps to reach a particular end point, the presentation of instructions and so on.

Using an Information Mapping methodology (or similar technique) is particularly important for web design because reading information off a screen is more difficult and more mentally fatiguing than from a paper document.

The method is both subject matter and media independent; that is, it can be applied to the subject matter of any industry, and it can be presented on paper, on a computer screen, verbally, or in a multimedia presentation.

Based on research into how the human mind actually reads, processes, remembers, and retrieves information, Information Mapping is an integrated set of easy-to-learn principles, techniques and standards. It enables authors to break complex information into its most basic elements and then present those elements optimally for readers. The result is a set of precisely defined information modules that are consistent from author to author and document to document.

Figure 2.11 is a typical example of an Information Map explaining how to prepare data for an audit.

The method is a basic tool that has been used successfully in a wide variety of documents in every industry. Any business or technical information – whether intended for initial communication, education, training, reference, quick reference, or performance support – will benefit from the method.

How to Prepare Data for an Audit

Introduction	One of the most important procedures in an audit is preparing the data. Careful preparation ensures that the data is correct and that each step of preparation has been carried out.
Procedure	Follow the steps below to prepare data for the audit.

Step	Action
1	For data items selected for the audit, obtain the following: • source document samples, *and* • run data from the computer room.
2	Verify the source document samples by comparing the samples to the original list.
3	Record on a worksheet sufficient descriptive information to provide accurate identification for future audits.

MINIMUM INFORMATION REQUIRED	EXAMPLES
Attributes of the sample	• Sales Territory • Effective data
Description of each data item	• Account Name • Account Number • Type of Business

Figure 2.11 Information Mapping Audit

2.3 Case Study: Industry collaboration via ISWorld Net

ISWorld Net (<http://www.isworld.org/>) is an entry point to resources related to information systems technology for information systems academics and practitioners. ISWorld Net is a WWW repository that serves a global community of Information Systems Faculty drawn from throughout the world. Repositories support teaching, research, and professional service.

Not based at just one location, ISWorld Net relies on volunteers, a consistent format, and an editorial evaluation structure. A distributed implementation scheme permits individual contributors to provide pages from their own servers located throughout the world. ISWorld Net was initially conceived and created by the Executive Director of CVOC International. It is hosted at Baylor University and mirrored at University College Dublin and Melbourne University (two CVOC partner universities).

It is styled to be both a knowledge repository and a learning community, allowing collaboration to occur through sharing of theory and distribution of information. It also provides positions available in the IS academic community and teaching aids for others to use in the classroom.

Why ISWorld Net works is through the efforts of volunteers who are motivated to share ideas and offer information to benefit both their own research efforts and those of future researchers just starting in the field.

Questions:

1. What kind of peer pressure allows ISWorld Net to be successful?
2. What technology is needed for participating in a collaborative portal such as this?

2.4 Key Terms

Decision Support: A decision support system (DSS) is a computer program application that analyzes business data and presents it so that users can make business decisions more easily. It is an ‘informational application’ (in distinction to an ‘operational application’ that collects the data in the course of normal business operation).

Groupware: The following definitions, the most commonly used, are presented by industry leaders:

- Intentional group processes plus software to support them – Peter and Trudy Johnson-Lenz, 1978
- A co-evolving human-tool system – Doug Englebart, 1988
- Computer-mediated collaboration that increases the productivity or functionality of person-to-person processes – David Coleman, 1992.

Groupware Applications: Vertical applications that use collaborative technologies to either enhance processes or support collaboration in a specific work environment.

Knowledge Filtering: A method or process of transforming information into useful knowledge. Knowledge conversion involves filtering existing resources to focus, amplify, condense, and link that material to the original source so that a user can easily assimilate the summary and determine whether direct access to the source material is required.

Knowledge Preservation: Storage of knowledge is a very important part of a knowledge-based system. During specific preservation of experience, information and documents require management efforts. In an enterprise, every day a mass of knowledge normally arises in the form of minutes, letters, presentations in widespread places, etc. The difficulty is to select between the knowledge items that are worth preserving, and those that are not (see also knowledge utilization). The main rule for this decision is the question whether others will use this knowledge. Otherwise, it would decrease the trust in the quality of the system. Knowledge preservation is a permanent process, which must be supported by continuous updating.

Multiparticipant Decision Maker (MDM): is an activity conducted by a collective entity composed of two or more individuals and characterized in terms of both the properties of the collective entity and of its individual members.

2.5 Review Questions

1. Describe how collaborative systems have evolved from the 'Semantic Web' description on page 46 to what they are today. What do they allow people to do in terms of sharing data, voice and multimedia?
2. Explain the role of interoperability in why certain groupware solutions have been successful or unsuccessful. Give one example of a groupware solution that has become an industry standard and why that has occurred, both technologically and in terms of the market.
3. What are the main technological benefits of GSS?

Chapter 3

CORPORATIONS AND NETWORKS

Introduction

The virtual organization is comprised of corporate partnerships, connected via networks: both physical and social networks. The corporation, as we know it, has evolved into a hierarchical structure with the option of flat, multilayered, or decentralized governance. The same cannot necessarily be said for networks. Network structure is based on a seven-layer OSI model, which allows interoperability across diverse network structures.

Learning Objectives of the Chapter

When you have completed this chapter, you should be able to:

- Understand the relationship between the OSI layer and how network elements integrate
- Analyze network alternatives (LAN, MAN, WAN) as applicable to the organizational need
- Discuss the Internet as a communication network.

3.1 Technology of Computer Networks and Integration into Corporate Campuses

3.1.1 OSI Model and Network Protocols

The OSI Reference Model of network architecture, and a suite of protocols (protocol stack) to implement it, were developed by ISO in 1978 as a framework of international standards in heterogeneous computer network architecture (Intrinsix, 2002). The architecture is split between seven layers, from lowest to highest:

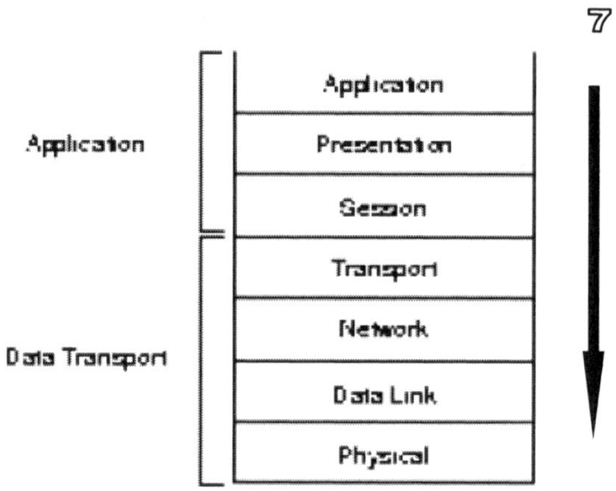

Figure 3.1 OSI Model

Each layer uses the layer immediately below it and provides a service to the layer above.

Layer 1 – Physical
Physical layer defines the cable or physical medium itself, e.g., thinnet, thicknet, unshielded twisted pairs (UTP). All media are functionally equivalent. The main difference is in convenience and cost of installation and maintenance. Converters from one media to another operate at this level.

Layer 2 – Data Link
Data Link layer defines the format of data on the network. A network data frame, a.k.a. packet, includes checksum, source and destination address, and data. The largest packet that can be sent through a data link layer defines the Maximum Transmission Unit (MTU). The data link layer handles the physical and logical connections to the packet's destination, using a network interface. A host connected to an Ethernet would have an Ethernet interface

to handle connections to the outside world, and a loopback interface to send packets to itself.

Ethernet addresses a host using a unique, 48-bit address called its Ethernet address or Media Access Control (MAC) address. MAC addresses are usually represented as six colon-separated pairs of hex digits, e.g., 8:0:20:11:ac:85. This number is unique and is associated with a particular Ethernet device. Hosts with multiple network interfaces should use the same MAC address on each. The data link layer's protocol-specific header specifies the MAC address of the packet's source and destination. When a packet is sent to all hosts (broadcast), a special MAC address (ff:ff:ff:ff:ff:ff) is used.

Layer 3 – Network

NFS, or the Network File System, was originally developed by Sun Microsystems in the 1980s as a way to create a file system on diskless clients. NFS provides remote access to shared file systems across networks. NFS uses Internetwork Protocol (IP) as its network layer interface. IP is responsible for routing, directing datagrams from one network to another. The network layer may have to break large datagrams, larger than MTU, into smaller packets and the host receiving the packet will have to reassemble the fragmented datagram.

The Internetwork Protocol identifies each host with a 32-bit IP address. IP addresses are written as four dot-separated decimal numbers between 0 and 255, e.g., 129.79.16.40. The leading 1–3 bytes of the IP identify the network and the remaining bytes identifies the host on that network. The network portion of the IP is assigned by InterNIC Registration Services, under the contract to the National Science Foundation, and the host portion of the IP is assigned by the local network administrators, locally by noc@indiana.edu. For large sites, usually subnetted, the first two bytes represents the network portion of the IP, and the third and fourth bytes identify the subnet and host respectively.

Even though IP packets are addressed using IP addresses, hardware addresses must be used to actually transport data from one host to another. The Address Resolution Protocol (ARP) is used to map the IP address to its hardware address.

Layer 4 – Transport

Transport layer subdivides user-buffer into network-buffer sized datagrams and enforces desired transmission control. Two transport protocols, Transmission Control Protocol (TCP) and User Datagram Protocol (UDP), sit at the transport layer. Reliability and speed are the primary difference between these two protocols. TCP establishes connections between two hosts on the network through 'sockets' that are determined by the IP address and port number. TCP keeps track of the packet delivery order and the packets that must be resent. Maintaining this information for each connection makes TCP a stateful protocol. UDP on the other hand provides a low overhead transmission service, but with less error checking. NFS is built on top of UDP because of its speed and statelessness. Statelessness simplifies the crash recovery.

Layer 5 – Session

The session protocol defines the format of the data sent over the connections. The NFS uses the Remote Procedure Call (RPC) for its session protocol. RPC may be built on either TCP or UDP. Login sessions uses TCP whereas NFS and broadcast use UDP.

Layer 6 – Presentation

External Data Representation (XDR) sits at the presentation level. It converts local representation of data to its canonical form and vice versa. The canonical uses a standard byte ordering and structure packing convention, independent of the host.

Layer 7 – Application

Provides network services to the end-users. Mail, ftp, telnet, DNS, NIS, and NFS are examples of network applications.

3.1.2 TCP/IP Network Model

Although the OSI model is widely used and often cited as the standard, the TCP/IP protocol has been used by most Unix workstation vendors. TCP/IP is designed around a simple four-layer scheme. It does omit some features found under the OSI model. Also it combines the features of some adjacent OSI layers and splits other layers apart (Indiana University , 1996).

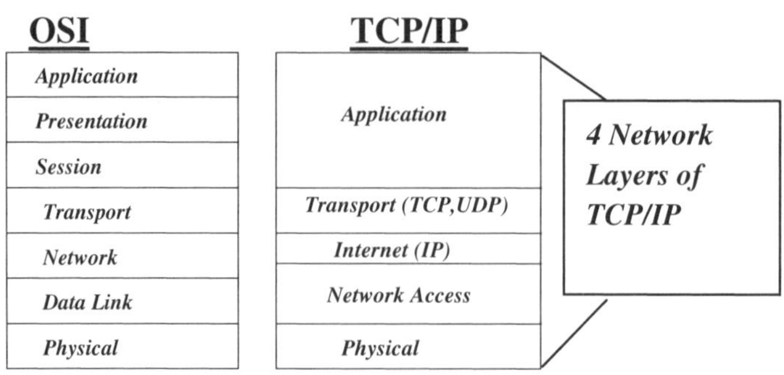

Figure 3.2 OSI and TCP/IP Stacks Compared

The four network layers defined by TCP/IP model are as follows.

Layer 1 – Link
This layer defines the network hardware and device drivers.

Layer 2 – Network
This layer is used for basic communication, addressing and routing. TCP/IP uses IP and ICMP protocols at the network layer.

Layer 3 – Transport
Handles communication among programs on a network. TCP and UDP falls within this layer.

Layer 4 – Application
End-user applications reside at this layer. Commonly used applications include NFS, DNS, arp, rlogin, talk, ftp, ntp and traceroute.

3.1.3 For Virtual Organizations, Why Does OSI Matter?

The OSI model and network protocols are the basis for how computer systems communicate with each other. In terms of the virtual environment, this is critical to exchanges of information, both data and voice.

Network Protocols are commonly defined as the formal description of a set of rules and conventions that govern how devices on the network layer (layer 3 of the OSI model) exchange information. Protocols provide the link by which systems connected to a network or internetwork may talk to each other. For two end systems to talk to each other, they must effectively ‘speak the same language’. This is usually done across a TCP/IP set of protocols for internetworking.

The Internet Protocol (IP) is a packet-based protocol used to exchange data over computer networks. IP handles addressing, fragmentation, reassembly, and protocol multiplexing. It is the foundation on which all other IP protocols, collectively referred to as the IP Protocol suite, are built (TCP, UDP, ICMP, ARP, etc.). IP is a network-layer protocol that contains addressing and control information that allows data packets to be routed.

The Transmission Control Protocol (TCP) is built upon the IP layer. TCP is a connection-oriented protocol that specifies the format of data and acknowledgments used in the transfer of data. TCP also specifies the procedures that the computers use to ensure that the data arrives correctly. TCP allows multiple applications on a system to communicate concurrently because it handles all multiplexing of the incoming traffic among the application programs.

Modems, Repeaters	– layer 1
Bridges, switches*	– layer 2
Routers*	– layer 3
Gateways*	– layers 1–7

*All use functionality of lower layers

Figure 3.3 Types of Network Devices used by Virtual Organizations

3.1.4 Area Networks: The Difference between LAN, WAN, and MAN

To create a communication mechanism between individuals, workgroups, departments, companies, campuses and regional areas, the appropriate size of network to cover that area is established.

LAN

The Local Area Network (LAN) is by far the most common type of data network. As the name suggests, a LAN serves a local area (typically the area of a floor of a building, but in some cases spanning a distance of several kilometers). Typical installations are in industrial plants, office buildings, college or university campuses, or similar locations. In these locations, it is feasible for the owning organization to install high quality, high-speed communication links interconnecting nodes. Typical data transmission speeds are one to 100 megabits per second.

A wide variety of LANs have been built and installed, but a few types have more recently become dominant. The most widely used LAN system is the Ethernet system developed by the Xerox Corporation.

Intermediate nodes (i.e. repeaters, bridges and switches) allow LANs to be connected together to form larger LANs. A LAN may also be connected to another LAN or to WANs and MANs using a 'router'.

In summary, a LAN is a communications network that is:

- local (i.e. one building or group of buildings)
- controlled by one administrative authority
- assumes other users of the LAN are trusted
- usually high speed and always shared.

WAN

The term Wide Area Network (WAN) usually refers to a network which covers a large geographical area, and uses communications circuits to connect the intermediate nodes. A major factor impacting WAN design and performance is a requirement that they lease communications circuits from telephone companies or other communications carriers. Transmission rates are typically 2 Mbps, 34 Mbps, 45 Mbps, 155 Mbps, 625 Mbps (or sometimes considerably more).

Numerous WANs have been constructed, including public packet networks, large corporate networks, military networks, banking networks, stock brokerage networks, and airline reservation networks. Some WANs are very extensive, spanning the globe, but most do not provide true global coverage. Organizations supporting WANs using the Internet Protocol are known as Network Service Providers (NSPs). These form the core of the Internet.

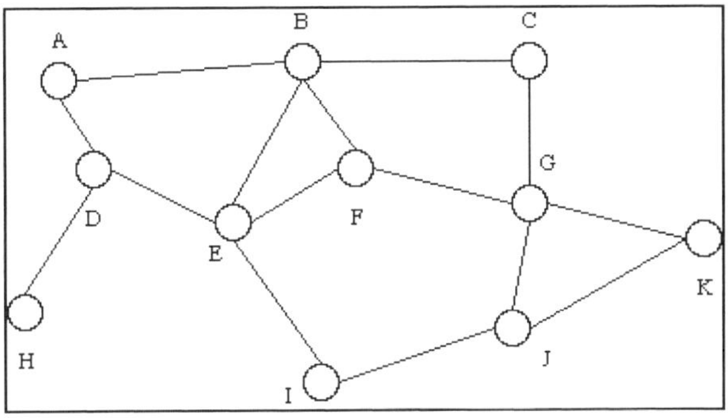

Figure 3.4 Typical "mesh" connectivity of a Wide Area Network

MAN

The definition of a Metropolitan Area Network (MAN) cannot be precise. It falls between a Local Area Network (LAN) and a Wide Area Network (WAN) and has some of the features of each. A MAN is a relatively new class of network: it serves a role similar to an ISP, but for corporate users with large LANs. There are three important features which discriminate MANs from LANs or WANs:

- The network size falls intermediate between LANs and WANs. A MAN typically covers an area of between 5 and 50 km diameter. Many MANs cover an area the size of a city, although in some cases MANs may be as small as a group of buildings or as large as the North of Scotland.
- A MAN (like a WAN) is not generally owned by a single organization. The MAN, its communications links and equipment is generally owned either by a consortium of users or by a single network provider who sells the service to the users. The level of service provided to each user must therefore be negotiated with the MAN operator, and some performance guarantees are normally specified.

- A MAN often acts as a high-speed network to allow sharing of regional resources (similar to a large LAN). It is also frequently used to provide a shared connection to other networks using a link to a WAN.

A set of computer interconnections becomes a *Network* when they have some form of common management. A LAN operates over restricted geographical areas and almost always operates within one organization. A number of LAN technologies have evolved offering very high performance at low cost over distances of less than 10 km. The WAN on the other hand uses technologies that do not limit the geographical reach and expects to connect nodes under different management domains. A MAN aims to serve a geographic area beyond the scope of LAN technologies, yet is restricted by some well-defined community of interest, often a city. A MAN will often provide interconnection between sites of the same organization as well as interconnecting organizations. This means that MANs have to provide performance close to that obtained on LANs yet cope with the interaction of multiple management domains. As a consequence, the establishment of a successful MAN requires the correct balancing of a number of technical and political factors.

Wireless LAN

A wireless Local Area Network (wLAN) connects to a network using two-way radio. The common standard for developing the technology is IEEE 802.11 and devices are sometimes described as using 802.11. The standard also details the encryption method. Wireless LANs comprise a wireless hub, or base station, and several wireless access cards. The wireless cards can communicate with the base station over hundreds of meters using radio waves. The base station will normally then connect to a wired Local Area Network or a modem/router, passing data on from the wireless to the wired network.

3.1.5 Communication Software and Network Management

Advances in communication software have enabled organizations to acquire and retain such distributed structures by supporting coordination among people working from different locations. A horizontal, rather than pyramid, structure not only allows greater worker empowerment, but also makes communicating vision throughout the organization an easier task. A flattened organization requires fewer managers, is less bureaucratic, and can produce more cross-functional employees. Advances in technology have not only flattened organizations, but also completely dissipated them.

The virtual organization is becoming the new dominant organization form. Virtual organizations can be defined as a temporary network of independent companies – suppliers, customers and rivals – linked by IT to share skills, costs and access to one another's market. The coordination of this organizational form is dependent on IT in order to overcome the limitations of time, space and stable organizational forms. Advancements in IT have made the virtual organization possible today.

The traditional organization considers choice of location to be an essential decision, made when the business is first established. It is primarily concerned with the search of the optimal place and structure to operate and produce goods and services. It does not take into account the management of distributed or mobile task accomplishment. Virtual and flat organizations use electronic mail and information technology to share information and coordinate their work. Use of e-mail allows these groups to call on expertise whenever needed regardless of where it resides. This use of e-mail enables a group to create and sustain its identity without a shared physical setting and enables existence of a group without visible participants.

To deal with the complexity of an ever-changing work environment, people need help in managing large quantities of information. This information is evolving dynamically and needs to be updated. Because information comes in such large quantities with archaic meanings, it is complex. Thus, the user needs ways of constructing views of the information, which display filtered and sorted subsets of the information in meaningful ways.

New forms of software support have been emerging which give people more power to manage their information. E-mail, videoconferencing, and real-time chats, and other types of groupware, have allowed people to communicate and share information effectively. An example is a popular peer-to-peer communication and collaboration tool in Microsoft's NetMeeting. Such tools provide significant potential for supporting people in flat organizations and other complex business situations. The basic function of these tools is to store and display multiple views of the information. In addition, well-designed software agents can add organizing and inferencing power, which creates views that provide new insights and perspectives for the user.

3.1.6 The Internet as a Communication Network

In examining the Internet using the resource-based theory of economics (RBT), one can say that the limited resources of the Internet are best allocated through market prices that reflect costs of production, consumption values, and opportunity costs of alternative uses. However, the Internet (as a communication network) does not have such 'market prices' even though it differs little from telephone networks or TV cable provisioning. The price one pays for Internet connection seldom corresponds to the actual cost or value of connection. Flat-rate pricing practices instead further distort resource allocation, often encouraging congestion.

Finding efficient prices for the Internet is difficult since a typical Internet connection involves such diverse networks as local telephone networks, long-distance fiber and satellite networks, and private wired as well as cable and wireless networks. Another factor is the legacy of the old NSF network, giving an impression that the Internet is essentially 'free'. The Internet is certainly not free; various organizations pay their share of the cost, but these shares are not allocated efficiently.

Contents distributed over the network, given inefficient connection pricing, have no economic prices (Choi *et al.*, 1997). Therefore an advertisement for an on-line flower shop competes with a critical medical database for delivery, and the former often wins. Because there is no agreed-upon market price or a way to pay and collect such payments, the Internet culture often relies on unenforceable moral standards (such as netiquettes) or threats of lawsuits (Choi *et al.*, 1997).

Inappropriate content such as spamming can be countered by technological means, such as filtering software; by legislation; or by a market mechanism. Some bills propose to ban spamming, equating e-mails with faxes. One approach could be to establish a system of legal on-line identity similar to identity cards in Europe, although this raises a privacy issue. Most troublesome spammers use unreturnable e-mail addresses, effectively avoiding backlash (Choi *et al.*, 1997). Similarly, Web-casting, like spamming, distributes contents without considering effective prices for network usage. These broadcast-based models appear reasonable only if we ignore economic prices (Choi *et al.*, 1997).

Protecting consumer privacy becomes extremely difficult when technologies are so advanced that the consumer's every move can be recorded and analyzed, with cookies, spyware and other mechanisms. Withholding identifiable information or regulating the use of such information may be one solution. Various cryptographic and technological means to hide information are another. But the issue of privacy will always be a part of Internet usage.

An active market for consumer information is deemed essential; it allows products to be personalized, a benefit of using information. An efficient market with established ownership rights over consumer information would allow, not limit, trading such a product. Many retail firms, on-line search services, and free e-mail providers are indeed in the business of commoditizing consumer information, albeit without encouraging consumer participation. Electronic commerce offers an opportunity to improve this imperfect information brokerage through market processes without an added burden of legal intervention (Choi *et al.*, 1997).

Subscription and bundling practices limit consumer choices and introduce inefficiency. Subscription and bundling, popular for physical products, may also be the preference in electronic commerce. As significant is the general trend toward unbundling, which is apparent even in physical markets (e.g., cable tiering, specialized magazines and journals). Greater options mean additional choices for consumers, increasing profits as an outcome. Giving consumers more choices requires a payment system flexible enough to bill for small or occasional purchases. With examples such as digital cash or smart money stored in smart cards, micropayment systems are essential in supporting need-based information trading in the Digital Age. Its alternative is wasted resources (like unwanted newspaper sections) or lowered quality (like broadcast messages catering to the lowest common denominator) (Choi *et al.*, 1997).

A more elemental issue regarding microtransactions stems from different visions about the future of information trading. Does anyone have the ability to become an information seller in the Digital Age? If so, selling bits of information and knowledge becomes impractical, if not impossible, without micropayments. But corporate players in software and entertainment industries see the Internet and electronic commerce as a 'revolutionary new market', and may dismiss millions of individual Web pages as clutter.

Some even predict that the wired and wireless information infrastructure will be used to sell entertainment and advertising rather than information and knowledge-based products. In this vision, the Internet is another telemarketing channel or a fancy television, and the need for micropayments is often dismissed (Choi *et al.*, 1997).

These comments show that choices in payment systems, technologies, and policies depend on how the future of electronic commerce is viewed. Our understanding of the nature of digital products and their uses is often influenced by what we know from physical markets. The global information infrastructure can open up a whole new market where the behavior of firms and consumers change will have existing policies and business practices evolving to the new way of business. We need to examine payment systems, as they are unique to the possibilities of the new electronic marketplace.

One question is if the 'Invisible Hand' of Adam Smith can regulate the electronic commerce market. Smith's belief in the economic system was based on his concept of human nature and the notion of the law-like universe; natural laws regulate economic activity/behavior. We are witnessing a wholly new type of market with far-reaching implications from production to consumption. Electronic commerce activities include on-line advertising and ordering and also consumer searches, digital production processes, intermediation and distribution, payment, product delivery, and consumption. The electronic marketplace is a virtual version of physical markets, with different time and space parameters.

As knowledge-based products become mainstream in the global economy, digital markets and electronic commerce will account for more of global economic activities than physical counterparts. People will still buy clothes and automobiles, but on-line custom tailors will offer better-fitting suits based on 3D scanning (Choi *et al.*, 1997). Smart automobiles equipped with smart cards will accept digital files for tune-ups, diagnosis and repair, travel directions and registration. Smart houses and smart appliances will be controlled via Web browsers or e-mail while you are vacationing. The list of digital products and services in the electronic marketplace could grow exponentially as the way we use knowledge and information evolves (Choi *et al.*, 1997).

Can the electronic marketplace be an improvement over physical markets? It may represent the most competitive and efficient market because the producers and buyers are in large numbers, transaction costs are therefore minimized, and information about products and prices is plentiful, although information asymmetry still exists. For such an efficient market to work, external interventions such as taxation and regulation should be avoided.

The unique properties of digital products might result in market dominance by only a few firms. Economies of scale, standardization, and network effects all might favor one software program over others, resulting in *de facto* monopolization. One example is the Office suite of Microsoft.

So should governments intervene to promote competition? What forms of market intervention will be effective? Requiring competing standards reduces efficiency, and it may punish good products and businesses. Regulation would not work when firms are not natural monopolies and face free entry. Breaking up vertically integrated firms may eliminate the ground for anti-competitive behaviors, but how should market boundaries be drawn? (Choi *et al.*, 1997). Governments, industries, and academic researchers all have roles to play in mapping out strategies for the 21st century.

3.1.7 Networked Applications

In delivering a keynote address at Comdex Fall 2001 in Las Vegas, Nevada, Cisco CEO John Chambers' message was clear: to thrive and survive in today's business world, companies need to harness the power of the Internet to yield productivity and profitability gains (Church, 2001).

The current business environment is focused on getting back to the core issues of profits, liquidity and cash flow, as well as productivity. What Cisco calls "Net Impact" is all about harnessing the power of networking to enable productivity applications that drive profits and cash flow. Companies require alliances to maintain a competitive edge, as they cannot do everything themselves. There is a need to outsource the elements of their business that lie beyond their core competencies and the best way to do this is to work within a networked ecosystem of partners. What is needed to achieve this is a correspondingly flexible business architecture to support this outsourced business model – one that aligns the business model and architecture to achieve optimum productivity. By creating improved productivity, value and more loyalty are obtained from customers. Networked applications are critical for any company interested in gaining competitive advantage in the Internet economy (Church, 2001).

In the Internet era, productive companies are those that streamline their business processes across their entire value chain or ecosystem. They develop and deliver those products and services that are 'core' to their business and outsource the context areas, or those that do not make financial sense to develop in-house. But this is a slow process, hindered by both technology and business standard practices.

To become a networked virtual organization, companies need to have both the necessary architecture and the internal or outsourced expertise. Becoming a networked virtual organization is not a process with a beginning and an end – it involves a constant cycle of investment and reinvestment in waves of applications. These waves of applications are what drive productivity payback, but the architecture is needed to support it (Church, 2001).

The applications that could possibly have a significant impact on productivity in the near future are the following: Virtual Private Networks (VPNs), Enterprise mobility and E-learning. The need to be constantly connected is becoming a requirement in the business world. Each of these applications allows people to be as productive out of the office as they are in the office. Anytime, anywhere access to corporate information and services from laptops, cell phones, pager and PDAs is the wave of the future.

A *VPN* (virtual private network) is commonly described as a way to use a public telecommunication infrastructure, such as the Internet, to provide remote offices or individual users with secure access to their organization's network. (Searchnetworking.com, 2003). A virtual private network can be contrasted with an expensive system of owned or leased lines that can only be used by one organization. The goal of a VPN is to provide the organization with similar capabilities, but at a lower cost.

A VPN works by using the shared public infrastructure while maintaining privacy through security procedures and tunneling protocols such as the Layer Two Tunneling Protocol (L2TP). Protocols, by encrypting data at the sending end and decrypting it at the receiving end, send the data through a 'tunnel' that cannot be 'entered' by data that is not properly encrypted. An additional level of security involves encrypting not only the data, but also the originating and receiving network addresses. There are a number of reasons to set up a VPN for remote access, but the biggest selling point by far is the potential cost savings.

Using the Internet to distribute network services over long distances means companies no longer have to purchase expensive leased lines to branch or partners' offices as a VPN connection needs only to use a relatively short dedicated connection. In an organization experiencing rapid growth, this can make an enormous difference in costs. As an organization adds companies to its network, the number of leased lines required climbs with it exponentially. In a traditional WAN, this can limit the flexibility for growth, whereas VPNs avoid this problem by tapping into an almost universally available network.

VPNs can further reduce costs by lessening the need for long-distance telephone charges, as clients can gain access by dialing into the nearest service provider's access point. While in some cases this may entail making a long-distance call or using a toll-free 800 service, a local call is usually sufficient. This can dramatically cut telecommunications costs for enterprises with many international sites, sometimes in the range of thousands of dollars per person, each month.

Yet another way that VPNs may result in lower expenditures is through reducing the company's support burden. With a VPN, the service provider must support dial-up access, instead of the organization using it. Theoretically, a public service provider can charge much less for support, because its cost is shared among a wider customer base.

VPNs can save a company on operational costs for equipment previously used to support remote users. A company using a VPN can get rid of its modem pools, remote-access servers, and other WAN equipment and simply use its existing Internet installation. Many companies employ several links with different functions prior to setting up a VPN.

VPNS can be used to allow enterprise mobility, enabling anywhere access to employees who are out of the office (and in the office), ensure real-time communication of action items that require immediate attention, and provide a more efficient means to bring products and services to market. In addition, many corporations are embarking on wireless initiatives designed to further embrace customers – from business travelers to students.

Enterprise applications need to be used over the VPN, such as Sales Force Automation (SFA) software that can provide customer history, product specifications, pricing and availability, terms and conditions, and competitive information. Customer relationship management (CRM) systems help to manage interactions with customers by improving sales, marketing, and customer support processes. Each part of an organization that has direct or indirect interaction with customers can benefit from real-time access to customer information.

Wireless extensions of back-end data leverage investments in Enterprise Resource Planning (ERP) software. All types of mobile workers can be armed with information from primary business applications including accounting and controlling; production and materials management; quality management and plant maintenance; sales and distribution; human resources; and project management. Wireless extensions of back-end data also leverage investments in Supply Chain Management (SCM) software and allow mobile workers to be even more responsive to business needs and make quicker, more informed decisions. Benefits include dramatically reducing lead times, accelerating order fulfillment, decreasing production downtime, reducing inventory, decreasing transportation costs, and increasing forecast reliability.

Virtual Physical Security (VPS) is important to provide the adequate security for the PC regardless of its location. Normal physical security measures, such as locked offices, alarm systems, and security guards, are the foundation for securing any computing device. When a PC is removed from a location secured by such measures, the basic foundation is removed as well, reducing the effectiveness of onboard security technologies. Having VPS enables an enterprise to securely use its mobile devices through scalable, centralized administration of disk encryption as well as flexible mandatory access control.

3.2 Virtual Networks in Corporations

IT places a critical role in the success of the flattened/virtual organization. IT has allowed virtual organizations to acquire and share information very expediently and in an organized fashion. IT and decentralized structures allow organizations to respond quickly and with great flexibility to dynamic and turbulent environments.

Virtual workgroups and extended supply chain participants can use encrypted communications between users. Both business-to-business and business-to-consumer services can be provided using trusted client security features. For example, secure work group files can be accessed on public Internet sites, but only read and used by authorized partners or users.

Nevertheless, technological advances alone are not sufficient to insure a virtual organization's success. Companies must undergo major social changes and standards for interaction (i.e., types of communication software, databases, etc.) and exchange of property (i.e., financial resources, currency, how to sign and approve things, etc.) must be developed and implemented for a virtual organization to be successful.

3.2.1 Learning and Communities of Practice

Learning is an internal process of taking in information and experience. Training is one of many means to facilitate learning. Training is appropriate when developing meta skills, when performance must be automatic, and competence is time-critical. Training cannot be seen as appropriate when what is changing is content, not performance.

By definition, *e-learning* must be a networked, Web-based platform, integrated into a broader architecture of solutions (Kaplan and Bartlett, 2002). The architecture includes training and non-training components. The components of the framework would include items such as:

1. online training,
2. performance support and software, and
3. knowledge of information design.

The concept of 'blending' is a combination of both classroom and online training, interspersed. E-learning has evolved to be more independent from traditional training organizations (mainly based on content) (Kaplan and Bartlett, 2002).

Most learning professionals today agree that 'community' represents an increasingly important trend in e-learning, blended learning, and ultimately, organizational learning. The challenge is that the meaning of 'community' has become ambiguous. Communities come by many names – learning communities, knowledge communities, e-communities, corporate communities, and communities of practice, among others. The concept is often further diluted through being equated to technology such as discussion boards and chat rooms (Kaplan and Bartlett, 2002).

The argument for building communities usually goes something like this: about 70% of what an employee needs to know is learned outside of formal training programs (e.g., on the job, through informal mentoring, through networks of personal relationships, etc.). Since organizations are increasingly reliant on distributed groups of employees and partners to get work done, a new approach for enabling learning and collaboration is now required. For learning professionals, the question usually is not whether building communities will benefit the organization, but rather what kind of community is appropriate and what are the steps involved in building it.

Therefore when creating collaborative learning communities, developers should consider more than just the technology. It should begin by clarifying the business objectives and how the strategy translates into group and individual competency requirements. From there, learning objectives may be defined that support competency gaps. But how is the need of the community defined?

According to Webster's Dictionary (1996), a community is "any group living in the same area or having interests, work, etc. in common". While the geographic assumption underlying this definition may no longer be valid, one thing is clear: communities can be small or large, co-located or online, and often possess similar structures and characteristics. Their members interact together over time, are held together by a common purpose, possess distinct roles, rely on trust as the basis of their interactions, and share a sense of history (Kaplan and Bartlett, 2002).

There are four types of collaborative groups that relate to the strategic objectives and responsibilities of many typical training functions (this assumes the broadest definition of the learning professional role, including stand-up trainer, e-learning architect, and organizational development consultant) (Kaplan and Bartlett, 2002). While by no means mutually exclusive, these four groups represent people who come together primarily for any one of four distinct reasons:

- to affiliate (affinity networks)
- to learn (learning communities)
- to practice (communities of practice)
- to take action (project teams).

These groups vary in their orientations toward relationship, learning, and task. All communities include some of each reason group, though their emphases vary. Affinity networks are 'specialized relational networks' that assist in linking with peers and other leaders in the area of interest. Affinity networks tend to be the most relationship-focused since their existence is predicated primarily on the common personal attributes and preferences of its members. Learning communities are focused on a specific learning outcome, with relationship and task a necessary part of achieving the learning outcome. Communities of practice represent a relatively equal mix of relationship, learning, and task orientation, while project teams are predominantly task-oriented, though relationships and learning are indeed important for bonding the team together (Kaplan and Bartlett, 2002).

Affinity networks are groups of people who are drawn together based on one or more shared personal attributes. Their activities are highly relationship-oriented, and typically include networking, mentoring, and representing a collective voice in both organizational and external community affairs. While some organizations formally acknowledge and sponsor these groups' activities, when they don't, these networks often emerge on their own. Employee clubs are often-used examples. Other examples include 'employee associations', such as at Pacific Gas and Electric Company (PG&E), which sponsors five employee groups including the Asian, Black, Filipino, Hispanic, and Lesbian/Gay/Bisexual associations. As a strategy to strengthen communications among and between employees and customers, PG&E supports these groups as they volunteer as translators in crises, raise scholarship money for women and minorities, participate in community outreach, and contribute to PG&E's diversity programs (Kaplan and Bartlett, 2002).

Learning communities are the most closely connected to traditional training. They represent communities of learners that may rely on face-to-face and/or online interactions to share experiences, stories, network, and learn from each other over time. For trainers and e-learning professionals, learning communities are one of the best opportunities to create 'blended solutions' that move learning beyond the classroom. Often facilitated by a trainer or consultant, these groups may come together both prior to and after a face-to-face event. The online community provides 'context' prior to the event and then allows for mentoring, collaboration, and closure following the in-person gathering. For example, Hewlett-Packard, prior to its Compaq acquisition, had extended its two-day executive leadership training to include an eight-week online forum for tracking leaders' progress toward learning goals (Kaplan and Bartlett, 2002).

Communities of practice (CoPs) are groups of people who possess a common interest in sharing, learning about, and advancing a specific domain of knowledge. According to the American Productivity and Quality Center, CoPs "are driven by a desire and need to share problems, experiences, insights, templates, tools, and best practices" (APQC, 2003). While certain CoPs focus on specific business functions, others are focused on building and diffusing knowledge across diverse groups of employees, or even across companies. SBC Pacific Bell, for example, provides both in-person training and an online community for almost 2000 affiliates involved in the sales of its telecommunications services. These key partners integrate SBC's offerings into broader telecom solutions for their clients and, subsequently, require the most current sales, support, and technical resources to be successful. SBC's online community supplements the face-to-face sales and support training offered to its affiliates by providing a secure web-based environment in which partners can access information, surface problems, connect with subject matter experts, and contribute and share best practices (Kaplan and Bartlett, 2002).

According to Gartner Group forecasts, virtual project teams will deliver 80% of all global knowledge work by 2005. Virtual teams are groups of people that work together but are physically apart. Their activities are often time-bound – they come together to accomplish a specific task and when their objective is met, they disband, with members joining other newly forming project teams. Unlike affinity groups or communities of practice, virtual teams often have a discrete lifespan that is tied to specific business deliverables. Learning professionals are faced with a significant opportunity to capture and diffuse process and content-related knowledge and best practices related to the activities of virtual teams. From a process perspective, the methodology for quickly and efficiently assembling, launching, building, managing, and reallocating virtual team resources is a growing capability critical for most organizations' success in the coming years (Kaplan and Bartlett, 2002). From a content perspective, ensuring that new knowledge is captured and shared across teams is essential for enabling organizations to continue to learn from successes and failures.

Whether building an affinity network, facilitating a learning community, coordinating a community of practice, or working with a project team, creating communities requires a multidisciplinary approach. Sensitivity to the interrelationship of learning, knowledge management, and organizational development (including knowledge of business strategy and group behavior) are critical. An understanding of how technology can play an enabling role in supporting the group is also important since most communities tend to rely on various online tools as a means of communication and knowledge sharing.

Learning communities are logical starting points for most training organizations. They can be sanctioned internally to the HR department and can be implemented from within the department as a natural extension of existing programs. Since many training functions have already incorporated some form of blended learning into their existing strategies, including community tools may not require much internal selling (Kaplan and Bartlett, 2002).

While learning groups may be the easiest to handle for training departments, creating communities of practice are more strategic in the contributions that they can make. The challenge with CoPs is that they can be difficult to build and manage – ongoing senior level business sponsorship is essential, and participation is usually voluntary.

Learning professionals must address a variety of issues that have implications for the readiness of their organizations to embrace communities. Some of the strategic questions and issues to consider include:

- Business Issues – What role does your group play in your organization – is your role strictly to deliver stand-up courses, or are you able to define how your company can become a 'learning organization'?

- Sponsorship Issues – Do you have relationships with business leaders across the organization that can help you overcome roadblocks to building communities across the organization?
- Capability Issues – Can you pull together people with skills in organizational development, e-learning, knowledge management, and technology to get the job done?
- Technology Issues – Are you able to influence or even drive business unit or enterprise technology decisions to support your strategic learning programs?

From a tactical perspective, different groups require different supporting processes and technologies. Learning professionals who are keenly aware of these differences can anticipate issues and challenges, and create and facilitate online environments targeted at achieving specific business objectives and providing a measurable return on investment (ROI) for the organization (Kaplan and Bartlett, 2002). But this requires good dialogue with the providers of the technology.

Learning professionals today are faced with many options for fostering collaborative learning. Any analysis by IS professionals should begin with an understanding of the context in which these technologies will be used, including the fundamental purpose that bonds the group together and how different supporting processes and technologies will contribute to achieving individual and group learning objectives (Kaplan and Bartlett, 2002).

Building communities as a learning strategy requires consideration of business-, political-, human resource-, and technology-related issues. While some learning professionals may be well positioned to build communities that span the organization and contribute to the strategic knowledge- and best-practice-sharing goals of the business, others may need to first build community into traditional delivery models (Kaplan and Bartlett, 2002).

3.2.2 Networks and E-Commerce: The Role of Trust

The use of networks across virtual organizations is based on trust, such as the trust between employees who have never met but who must nevertheless rely on one another to accomplish a specific task; or the trust between on-line consumers and businesses. In e-commerce, the use of networks has been discussed in terms of a guarantee of the security and privacy of transactions for customers. The secure solution is seen in similar terms: some combination of data encryption and legal regulatory policy to ensure the integrity of transmitted data and prevent its misuse by unintended recipients (Fukuyama, 2002).

But in order to ensure both data is kept private and that a user receives a quality product, users need to do more than merely verify the identity of the person at the other end of the wire. Users need to assess the competence, reliability and reputation of the product or service. In today's world, commerce is extended globally over the Internet as an extension of the branding process for the range of services and products available. Therefore since the organizations are separated by even greater distances and cultural barriers, electronic shoppers need the reassurance of brands (Fukuyama, 2002).

The problem, of course, is one of trust. Merriam Webster's Online Dictionary (2003) defines trust as "assured reliance on the character, ability, strength, or truth of someone or something; one in which confidence is placed." It is difficult for trust in someone you have never met, or a company who you have never heard of in terms of reputation.

But even when companies or individuals interview the service-provider in person, we often do not have enough information to make an informed decision (Fukuyama, 2002). The problem is not verifying identities or backgrounds, as most services advertising in the phone book are legitimate businesses, but the subtle issue of quality. But how difficult then does the problem become when we have to make these evaluations over a cable modem pipeline, or corporate broadband pipes?

Corporate network, firms and institutions exist to provide a stable framework of norms and rules by which their members can interact with one another. These rules are what create trust, regardless of type of communication – physical or cyber. Digital networks exist in cooperation with social networks, rather than replacing them.

One of the real opportunities created by virtual networks and digital commerce is the potential for creating new intermediaries into the process of branding. Firms do not have to establish their own reputations for quality and reliability when branding can be provided by third parties (Fukuyama, 2002).

What kind of benefits can a virtual network provide to help an organization? According to a March 2000 report on trends in corporate training by W.R. Hambrecht & Co., "Corporate e-learning is one of the fastest growing and, we believe, most promising markets in the education industry". One example of corporate learning technology used for corporate benefit was the satellite advanced uplink facilities and broadband satellite network used in 2000 to distribute 30 hours of live coverage of Procter & Gamble's (P&G) Innovation 2000 technology fair at the Cincinnati Convention Center directly to more than 10,000 employee desktops around the world (Loral, 2000).

The three-day e-learning event, which was held June 13–15, 2000, was seen live by P&G employees in North America, South America and Europe, and on a delayed digital feed in Asia. During P&G's Innovation 2000, employees around the globe were able to 'virtually' visit the booths of more than 115 P&G presenters and vendors, hear keynote speeches, and see presentations and demonstrations on how to use the latest technologies to do their jobs more efficiently, effectively and productively. This multi-functional 'Technology Trade Show' focused on innovations in products, packaging and services, and it enabled connections across P&G's business areas and vast scientific and technical base, as well as with outside suppliers, research institutions and other technology providers (Loral, 2000).

P&G produced the video content, encoding the content into an internet protocol (IP) encapsulated format and sending the IP stream over dedicated T1 circuits from Cincinnati to the Loral CyberStar satellite uplink facility in New Jersey. The IP stream was then broadcast to a network of 19 sites worldwide. CyberStar satellite antennas, receivers and specific software located at these sites permitted end users to view the program using industry-standard Microsoft Media Player software directly on the desktop or in dedicated meeting rooms throughout the world (Loral, 2000).

The time, cost and efforts to reproduce this event physically at several locations, plus the benefit of allowing disparate employees to interact, cannot be adequately measured in today's metrics to the cost of the event.

Most discussions of the 'virtual network' focus on the negative aspects of security between parties in a virtual arrangement. Not enough focus on the benefits of working across a virtual network in terms of learning and communication.

3.3 Case Study: Cisco's E-Learning: Fortifying A Solid Environment

The ability to use corporate networks to teach, train, collaborate, and communicate – any time, anyplace – is changing the way companies learn, operate, and compete. E-learning is one of the most prominent applications benefiting from the convergence of network technologies. Convergence is a term used to describe the integration of many types of information – voice, video, text, graphics, images, and traditional alphanumeric data – onto the same network. These applications have helped leading organizations achieve quantifiable, bottom-line business benefits: reduced cycle times, more rapid product introductions, increased operating efficiency, rapid acquisition of new competencies and skills for employees and even customers or business partners, and better relationships with customers.

The simplest e-learning application may be nothing more than a set of PowerPoint slides, viewed with audio explanations, that is accessed on the World Wide Web. Here, simple graphical data in the form of slides is augmented by a modest low-bandwidth audio stream of a few kilobits per second (kbps). At the high end, e-learning applications may be based on two-way, full-motion video and voice streams interconnecting several remote locations and corporate desktops. With each video stream consuming between a few hundred kilobits and several megabits per second (Mbps), this application places special requirements on the network.

The technology requirement for an e-learning solution is an environment with a solid network foundation that is scalable to address the growth of users, highly available to meet their demands, and secure to ensure confidentiality when necessary. Given the current economic climate, with cost reductions, bottom-line pressures and time limitations of employees, the benefit of education at your seat, so to speak, is both quantitative in terms of cost and qualitative in terms of intangible time savings.

Cisco provides e-learning solutions to companies, and also itself considers e-learning as a horizontal foundation building block that helps cultural and social transformation take place. Once people experience e-learning, they will come to recognize that this may be the fastest, easiest way to get the information that they need to be successful with their customers. Cisco encourages its own employees to use e-learning by:

- Making e-learning non-threatening with an anonymous testing and scoring process that focuses on helping people improve rather than penalizing those who fail.
- Giving those who fail the tests precision learning targets (modules, exercises, or written materials) to help them pass and remove the fear associated with testing.
- Providing the ability for people to track, manage and ensure employee development, competency change, and ultimately performance change.
- Offering additional incentives and rewards such as stock grants, promotions, bonuses, and awards to employees who pursue specialization, certification, and qualifications earned with the help of e-learning.
- Adding a strategic top-down metric for Cisco executives, who are measured on their deployment of it.

Questions:

1. What might be the most effective ways to reach your audience via e-learning? Is a traditional slide show the best approach?
2. What business problem might a company be trying to solve? How does e-learning potential solve these problems?

3.4 Key Terms

LAN: A local area network (LAN) is a group of computers and associated devices that share a common communications line or wireless link and typically share the resources of a single processor or server within a small geographic area (for example, within an office building).

MAN: A metropolitan area network (MAN) interconnects users with computer resources in a geographic area or region. The term is applied to the interconnection of networks in a city into a single larger network (which may then also offer efficient connection to a wide area network). It is also used to mean the interconnection of several local area networks by bridging them with backbone lines.

OSI: OSI (Open Systems Interconnection) is a standard description or *reference model* for how messages should be transmitted between any two points in a telecommunication network. Its purpose is to guide product implementors so that their products will consistently work with other products. The reference model defines seven layers of functions that take place at each end of a communication. Although OSI is not always strictly adhered to in terms of keeping related functions together in a well-defined layer, many if not most products involved in telecommunication make an attempt to describe themselves in relation to the OSI model. It is also valuable as a single reference view of communication that furnishes everyone a common ground for education and discussion.

Developed by representatives of major computer and telecommunication companies beginning in 1983, OSI was officially adopted as an international standard by the International Organization of Standards (ISO). Currently, it is Recommendation X.200 of the ITU-TS.

VPN: A virtual private network (VPN) works by using the shared public infrastructure while maintaining privacy through security procedures and tunneling protocols. It can be contrasted with an expensive system of owned or leased lines that can only be used by one organization. The goal of a VPN is to provide the organization with the same capabilities, but at a much lower cost.

VPS: Virtual private security (VPS) includes disk encryption, access control and other methods of securitizing mobile devices.

WAN: A wide area network (WAN) is a geographically dispersed telecommunications network, much broader than a local area network

(LAN). A wide area network may be privately owned or rented, but the term usually connotes the inclusion of public (shared user) networks.

3.5 Review Questions

1. What is the relationship between the OSI layer and how network elements integrate together?
2. Your manager wants to install a network for your organization. Explain the different network options (LAN, MAN, WAN) as applicable to the organizational need.
   a) The group resides in one building, but interacts with suppliers in another portion of the same geographic area.
   b) The group exists in many buildings, but across a different geographic area.
3. How is the Internet seen and used as a communications network. What are the security challenges of this for an organization? What are the reliability challenges of this for an organization?
4. How technologically does the Internet enable a community of practice, as defined in the chapter?

Chapter 4

OVERALL VIRTUAL CONCERNS

Introduction

Due to its virtual nature, a virtual organization's success hinges on assuring parties in the relationship that their use of network services is secure and reliable, that their transactions are safe, and that they will be able to verify important information about transactions and transacting parties. The security, reliability, legal responsibility, and priorities of individuals, groups and corporations are discussed in this chapter.

Learning Objectives of the Chapter

When you have completed this chapter, you should be able to:

- Compare the security issues of a traditional organization to a virtual one
- Understand the management challenges of a virtual organization
- Examine how priorities for an organization may not correspond with the individual.

4.1 Security: Technical and Managerial Aspects of Collaboration

What is unique about virtual organizations when it comes to security? First of all, compared to a traditional organizational structure, these organizations have vague boundaries and independently administrated business units. Cooperation and coordination of efforts is dependent on relationship management and command, control, communication, and intelligence (C^3I) activities.

Virtual organizations include vendors and external partners early in the process – from product design through delivery and support. Competitors sometimes cooperate to complement each other's capabilities (McConnell, 2002). The defense industrial sector is a classic example: multiple manufacturers collaborate on contracts because of project size, complexity, and the need for multiple specialized services. One manufacturer may partner with another that is also collaborating with its competitors. An automotive supplier producing seats could be working with a few competing auto manufacturers on future designs. Such a business model means that company outsiders need greater access to information traditionally held within organizational boundaries.

In his classic study of American business, The Visible Hand, Alfred Chandler discusses "why the visible hand of management replaced the invisible hand of market mechanisms." (Miller and Engemann, 1997). One reason is that internalizing activities of many business units within a single enterprise, which required a managerial hierarchy, produced higher productivity, higher profits and lower costs than market mechanisms. This hierarchy, he observes, is what distinguishes the modern business enterprise from federations of autonomous units which "could not lower costs through increased productivity [and] ... could not provide the administrative coordination that became the central function of the modern business enterprise."

The need for a security structure within a productive virtual organization is to counter the urge of both internal and external parties to reduce that productivity and administrative coordination.

The information security models prevalent in most organizations are point-defense solutions that protect the perimeter because in the past,

- organizational boundaries were clearly defined,
- securing the perimeter was much easier than securing every system, and
- only insiders were considered trustworthy.

This model has been turned 180 degrees: virtual organization boundaries are often amorphous, defense of a changing and largely unknown perimeter is impossible, and insiders cannot necessarily be trusted. For instance, the FBI reports that insiders commit as much as 75 percent of all cyber crime – and this assessment is based only on reported security breaches (McConnell, 2002).

Without clear role definitions, companies must develop a broad set of rules and constantly evolving roles, which can result in higher administrative overhead. The emergence – or recognition – of the insider threat has driven many companies to create complex rule sets that completely segregate users, not only keeping 'inside outsiders' out of proprietary areas, but also screening much of the information used by their partners from true insiders. This can be built into the software and/or into the access network.

The need for security is particularly acute when high-speed internets are used to combine widespread computational resources into 'computational grids.' A computational grid is a distributed computing infrastructure for advanced science and engineering applications (Foster and Kesselman, 1999). A user can make use of and combine heterogeneous resources from many different locations in such a system in order to solve complex problems and better utilize existing resources. The grid software may abstract the distributed nature of the system to a level where the user can view the whole grid as one expansive virtual computer. At such a high level of abstraction the user does not need to worry about the location or even the type and number of resources being used by its applications.

Therefore security solutions providers can no longer afford to focus on border security. Tools such as firewalls, virus scanners, and intrusion detection systems are rapidly maturing, but rapid technology advances, a plethora of nonsecure products, and the growing complexity of corporate networks diminish their effectiveness. To appropriately respond to their increased vulnerability, virtual corporations must focus on building a layered defense to secure the information assets (McConnell, 2002). Figure 4.1 shows the three steps of an in-depth defense plan.

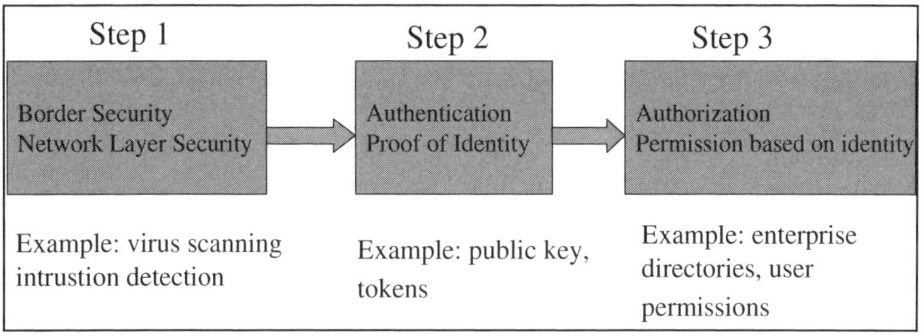

Figure 4.1. A layered defense allows an appropriate set of users to access the network and provides robust security throughout the extranet (Adapted from McConnell, 2002).

Secure access control needs to be established, enabling one central security scheme to be maintained for a distributed enterprise network. At the core of the security foundation is the enterprise directory (user information store). With effective directory services, the organization can consolidate, improve and use all user information to its advantage and at the same time, ensure that the data is secure.

There are several possibilities for an enterprise directory – either Microsoft Active Directory, a specialized product such as Oblix NetPoint, or utilizing a currently existing directory solution, whether it is open or proprietary.

Leveraging the information within the directory, the identity management solution can include permission and policy management, strong authentication, and provisioning, all driven by the power of workflow. Once this comprehensive identity management solution is in place, everything from authentication, authorization, management and security can be leveraged across the enterprise and scaled as necessary.

The kinds of security actions that need to be addressed in a virtual organization can include:

- Privacy through encryption.
- Content assurance: guaranteeing that transmissions have not been altered between sender and receiver.
- Source validation: verifying message source for legitimate processing.
- Authentication: establishing authorization for network and system privileges.
- Cross-application consistency: enabling security software to be consistently installed for a variety of applications without restricting transaction, communication, or processing activity.
- Hostile code protection: sandboxing (i.e., installing access controls) applications by allowing only certified entry to critical resources.

Virtual organizations can be compared to extranets, set up to allow suppliers and major customers access for streamlining of value chain activities. From experience in industry, it can be seen that use of extranets can pose the following risks:

- By allowing extranet Web servers access to internal databases, businesses have to make an opening in their firewall. The more openings a company has in its firewall, the greater the possibility for the wrong people to get in and do damage to internal systems and data.
- Too many extranet connections provide the potential entry points for computer viruses and other malicious code that can wreak havoc on information and information systems.
- An extranet connection often allows access to the company's proprietary data and therefore affords another avenue of access for unauthorized users to exploit sensitive or proprietary information.
- Because an extranet increases the number of network connections, it increases the risk of networking penetration. Once one network is compromised, an entry point for compromise of systems and data exists for all the other networks connected to it (Herold and Warigon, 1998, p.35).

- Should the extranet crash or become compromised due to lack of adequate security, the extranet operator may be held liable for the loss of business operations at other companies.
- If connecting partners to the extranet have inadequate access controls or have a lack of understanding of extranet security policies and requirements, they could expose the interconnected networks to penetration (Herold and Warigon, 1998, p.35).
- If connecting partners use modems to connect into the company, the potential exists for criminals to use war dialers or other means to dial into the network to access sensitive information or damage the network itself (Herold and Warigon, 1998, p.35).

To mitigate against these risks, security measures must be identified and implemented which protect the extranet connection throughout its life cycle. The life cycle of the extranet involves planning, implementing, and maintaining the connection. Security measures also must address the changing and evolving security vulnerabilities and threats to the systems and data accessed via the extranet.

Trust and decision making is based on relationship management and the level of control within the business unit and its function as a part of the relationship. Entitlement is a critical part of the architecture, but it is just one aspect (Munro, 2003). Therefore, it is critical to identify the key stakeholders that have a vested interest in defining enterprise security standards. Once identified, build an understanding of their key issues and value drivers. Only then will you be able to align the security with the business needs, and obtain the buy-in necessary for enterprise deployment.

4.2 Reliability and Responsibility of Technology

Virtual organizations do not exist within predefined physical or organizational boundaries, but rather exist as networks of interlocking relationships in response to changing demands in the marketplace. Dess *et al.* (1995) define virtual organizations as consisting "of a grouping of units of different firms that have joined in an alliance to exploit complementary skills in pursuing common strategic objectives". We may contrast virtual organizations with modular organizations that outsource activities but maintain strategic control because virtual organizations give up part of their control.

The factors causing virtual organizations to form existed long before the age of computers. For example, in the construction and movie industries groups of independent operators formed to build houses or to produce films. What has changed is that the trends that have led to virtual enterprises have increased. Bleeker (1994) reviews four such trends: First is pace. This is witnessed by compressed life cycles for all activities in the value chain and hierarchical organizations that cannot respond to new demands. Second is cost, especially the cost of market entry where small undercapitalized companies can now exert impact far beyond the apparent limits of their size. Third is customization: computerized manufacturing has made it possible to manufacture products with product runs of a few dozens or less. Besides not needing large manufacturing facilities to capture economies of scale, customization allows organizations to produce tailored products for many different customers. Fourth is globalization, where the competition includes firms throughout the world rather than in one local area. Taken together, these factors in many instances have made a hierarchical organization an inappropriate solution to the market's needs and have made virtual organizations viable options.

Perhaps most important is information technology, which underlies all of these trends by enabling an organization to gather, integrate, analyze, and disseminate large amounts of information quickly and accurately to consumers throughout the world. Without information technology virtual organizations could exist, as general contractors and subcontractors have existed for generations in the housing industry, but its scope and the areas in which it operates would be limited by time and space constraints. The Internet and its progeny are a specific form of information technology that has and will increasingly enable virtual organizations by allowing timely and ubiquitous access to large amounts of information in varied formats. Because of the uncertainty of how the Internet will evolve, one cannot say what its impact will be other than that impact will be great and profoundly affect the virtual organizations ongoing form and operations.

4.2.1 Management Functions

Because virtual organizations are organized quickly, for special functions, and are ephemeral, they affect classical management functions differently than hierarchical organizations that have been the seedbed for much of the development of management theory. The following discusses how virtual organizations differ from more traditional forms, and highlights the special demands and constraints that virtual organizations place upon those within them.

4.2.2 Strategic Reach

Virtual organizations extend strategic reach, which involves enlarging the scope and scale of opportunities available to the organization. Three examples concern size, time, and place. Many organizations, limited by size of lack of capital, cannot take advantage of emerging business opportunities. Miller *et al.* (1993) discuss Rosenbluth Travel, a firm with sales of $40 million in 1980, who by creating a global virtual network of travel agencies achieved revenues of over $1.3 billion by 1993. Their capital would never have allowed them to achieve this growth, but by forming a virtual organization with global affiliates, they created a network offering services that no one member could have offered by itself. Entering into a virtual network expands the organization's capabilities and allows it to be a player in markets where size constraints had previously excluded it.

Time is a second strategic constraint that a virtual network can overcome. Going virtual enables the firm to respond more quickly and mobilize to take advantage of market opportunities. For example, Upton and McAfee (1996) discuss an Internet-based electronic bidding system implemented by McDonnell in a virtual factory. They estimate the cost savings by the bidding alone pay for the operating cost of the entire factory management system. Acting as a stand-alone firm, this may be impossible even for the most well-positioned organizations such as McDonnell.

Place is the third example of how virtual organizations have a wider strategic reach. Place can include the ability to enter into previously closed markets, or to offer products in the marketspace, rather than the marketplace (Rayport and Sviokla, 1995). Marketspace products create value with information; once set up, they offer the opportunity to offer products with zero or minimal marginal costs.

Underlying the above examples is the concept of breaking scale, scope, time, and place constraints. What this does is increase a firm's strategic options and broaden the strategic horizon, enabling the firm to consider and take advantage of more strategic opportunities. The benefits of this are obvious. Greater opportunities mean greater returns if those opportunities are chosen wisely. What this does, however, is place more pressure on the organization to search out opportunities, to find partners, and to evaluate what opportunities it does and does not want to accept.

4.2.3 Technological Leverage

Organizations participating in virtual networks can leverage their technological capabilities by incorporating the capabilities of their partners. Doing this can enhance their technological presence and enable them to take advantage of previously ignored business opportunities. However, by depending on other firms' technologies, or by specializing in one aspect of a technology in hopes of complementing its partners' technologies, a firm risks ceding technological control and risking permanent technological atrophy (Chesbrough and Teece, 1996). For example, the aforementioned authors discuss the case of IBM's development of the IBM PC, where IBM allowed third parties to develop important pieces of the architecture in a virtual alliance, and thus gain expertise. As events played themselves out, the alliance partners did not follow IBM's lead on future developments and IBM could not stop them from following Microsoft's lead when it introduced Windows rather than follow IBM with its OS/2 operating system.

The risk organizations face when forming alliances with other firms to leverage their technologies, is that over time, whatever technological edge the organization has may disappear. The lesson for an organization in this situation is to constantly monitor and assess technologies and keep itself technologically proficient. This need not mean being a technological jack-of-all-trades, but requires maintaining technological expertise in certain key technologies deemed important. By following this process, rather than risking being passed by, the organization's technological expertise make it more attractive to potential partners and expand the scope of its opportunities.

4.2.4 Organizational Complexity

By extending an organization's global reach, virtual organizations encounter new organizational complexities. Many of these issues are similar to issues encountered by hierarchical organizations with global operations, but the network's virtual nature diminishes the ability for centralized focus and control.

Three examples are employee practices, labor policies and cross-border data flows. Employees working for virtual organization either are employees of the partners comprising the network or individuals hired to work on a contract basis for one of the partners. Relevant issues include: How the employees' capabilities fit the requirements of the virtual enterprise; telecommuting when employees do not work at a partners' site; and monitoring employee performance. The level of supervision in a virtual enterprise, especially for telecommuters, is less than in traditional organizations and the virtual organization must establish policies and practices to deal with this to ensure effective operations. Kirk (1996) discusses some downside risks telecommuting arrangements.

The second example is labor practices, which vary among countries and in many countries are significantly different from and usually less stringent than practices in advanced economies. These practices include working conditions and may also include child labor. While hierarchical organizations may have policies to control suppliers, practices for virtual organizations may be less well defined and may lead to disagreements among the virtual enterprises' partners. The result, beyond the immediate effects to the individuals involved, is embarrassment and potentially other damaging legal and image implications for one or more members of the virtual alliance.

Cross-border data flows are a third issue. For global virtual enterprises, these flows occur frequently and in environments with inherently looser controls than those faced by established hierarchical organizations. As with labor practices, in some countries firms may inadvertently engage in activities that may be illegal and which may result in unforeseen repercussions.

4.2.5 Organizing the Virtual Partners

Creating virtual alliance requires selecting the right partners and establishing a functional organization composed of all alliance members. Because issues of strategy and control come into play, organizing for a virtual alliance means knowing the expertise of the affiliated organizations and some foreknowledge of the compatibility among all of the organizations. Beyond the ability to work together, this includes compatible organizational cultures, resource availability at the proper times and place, technological capabilities and the financial strength of the alliance partners. Because partners in virtual alliances are diverse, using standards may ensure uniformity.

Besides organizing for ongoing operations, virtual organizations must organize for innovation. Chesbrough and Teece (1996) indicate that when faced with rapid technological change, large companies may profit from virtual alliances rather than face competition from smaller more agile competitors with more technological expertise. However, when innovation is systemic, that is, when it depends on a series of interdependent innovations, an organization should stay within its boundaries rather than use a virtual framework. Though large companies were mentioned, this principle holds true for any company with expertise greater than its alliance partners.

4.2.6 Leadership

Leadership in a virtual organization occurs in a different environment than that of hierarchical, command and control organization. Teamwork replaces hierarchy and leadership becomes more collaborative and takes on attributes enunciated by Deming (1991). Rather than be a judge, leaders in a virtual organization are more colleagues and counselors. This is true because of the nature of the virtual enterprise and also because of the inability to judge employees, often separated by distance and inter-organizational barriers. Because of the varying capabilities of the virtual organization's participants, leadership may evolve along different dimension, with various individuals or firms taking the lead role depending on the issue. However, the lack of focus or central responsibility creates new risks. To address these risks, even when distributing leadership, virtual organizations should maintain a central focus for accountability. Practically speaking, this involves identifying one of the virtual participants, usually from the virtual partner 'more equal' than others, as having the lead responsibility on a particular enterprise. Failure to define a single point of focus can cause the enterprise to flounder, especially when the participants work on many virtual projects.

4.2.7 Coordination and Control

As mentioned above, Chandler says the problems of coordinating the activities of autonomous units is a reason for the growth of the hierarchical organization. A managerial hierarchy provides the mechanism to facilitate information flows, from bottom to top, top to bottom, and horizontally within organizational units. These information flows are necessary to facilitate the increasingly complex coordination and control mechanisms required to deliver goods and services to customers and, as Applegate (1995) indicates, require that the organization's management processes must be aligned with its operating processes.

Virtual organizations have several barriers to coordination and control. First, virtual organizations often are transitory, and the control culture and control systems for the virtual network may be different or non-existent. Second, because of time and place differences, implementing any control system for the virtual alliance may be problematic, even when all the participants of the alliance agree on its form. Moreover, these same differences make collecting, aggregating, reporting, and analyzing information difficult. Third, members of a virtual alliance may be partners in one venture but competitors in others. Thus, they have less incentive to be open and share data than would departments within hierarchical organizations or within alliances of suppliers and customers.

The management process of coordination and control in virtual organizations is multidimensional. Virtual organizations must coordinate and control activities of units from different organizations. These are often located in different places, therefore virtual organizations can use different information systems and telecommunications networks to achieve objectives where time is a critical factor. In addition, the virtual environment often means there is no informal network of relationships among the managers that has evolved over time, in contrast with traditional organizations, as shown in Figure 4.2. Finally, participants in virtual enterprises have loyalties to the enterprise but more loyalty to their parent company. This exacerbates coordination and control issues, already present among functions in vertically integrated companies, by adding yet another dimension and another potential impediment to the free flow of information.

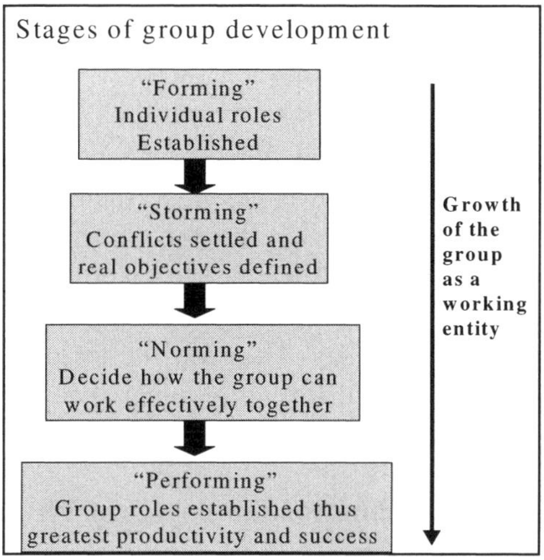

Figure 4.2. Stages of group development in a virtual organization

Information technology makes virtual organizations possible because it enables coordination and control, and makes feasible processing large amounts of timely and accurate information. Whereas in hierarchical organizations many levels of managers process and disseminate information to coordinate and control the organization's activities, in virtual organizations the participants coordinate and control these activities themselves. Two success factors involve technologies and people.

Information and decision technologies can improve decision-making throughout the organization by providing information that is accurate, comprehensive, and timely. Examples of these technologies include the Internet and groupware, such as Lotus Notes. Decision support and executive information systems allow senior managers to access information at lower levels of the organization and allow employees at lower levels to access environmental information previously unavailable, and to share information with each other.

Regarding people, Applegate (1995) says that information-age organizations must rethink the nature of authority. The tradeoff no longer is one of autonomy vs. control, i.e. decentralization vs. centralization, but rather involves authority being vested in teams. This requires developing a new set of management and decision-making skills, for example, in leadership, negotiation, and decision-making methods. In virtual organizations these teams may be 'virtual' in that they are physically separate. Because of the lack of physical proximity, employees of virtual organizations often have more autonomy that do those in hierarchical organizations, which makes coordination and control even more complicated. This requires trust because as Handy (1995) points out, "You manage people you don't see by trusting them."

Chesebrough and Teece argue that history indicates that coordination is more successful when carried out by companies who remain at the center of the network and use that position to leverage their capabilities. Although their examples concern enterprises in the pre-information systems age, the lessons may be equally relevant to virtual enterprises. "While business conditions have certainly changed, many of the principles that worked a century ago still pertain," they say. They say the lesson for firms in virtual alliances is to maintain strategic leverage, rather than relying on excessive decentralization and outsourcing.

4.2.8 Technology Implications for Employees of Virtual Organizations

Speed and customization, two themes behind virtual products, also provide a framework to analyze how working in a virtual organization affects employees. The virtual environment affects employees in three ways: personally, organizationally, and technologically. Each of these dimensions places new requirements on employees and demands new skills from them.

Employees working in virtual organizations face ambiguities in their relationships among fellow employees; relationships between the employee, employer and the virtual organization; and questions regarding functional and organizational career growth. These issues can be problematic even in hierarchical organizations where the organizational boundaries are clear and employees often are 'protected' from the ambiguities of the virtual enterprise.

Employees who work in virtual offices lose the interpersonal contact their counterparts in traditional offices have. This may lead to losing: a sense of community with other employees; the drama from being 'on-site'; a feeling of connectedness to the company; and the contact with others necessary to evaluate other employees and be evaluated by other employees (Connelly 1995). Even when employees in the organization do not telecommute, many of these issues still are relevant, particularly those concerning long-term relationships among individual worker and between workers and the organization.

Requirements for speed and customization and advances in telecommunications technologies can cause employees always to be 'on call'. Trends toward customization can cause excessive focus on responding to customers' demands, either directly or through intermediaries. Because the virtual organization is ephemeral, the employee does not have the job security present in hierarchical corporations although, even there, job security is quickly eroding given ongoing trends in corporate downsizing. What is different is that employees of virtual organizations may not have the support system of other employees and relationships among superiors in the organization to draw on when demands become excessive.

Long-term evaluation of employees also is an issue. For managers in virtual organizations, how does one evaluate subordinates one sees irregularly and subordinates housed in other parent organizations? Evaluation always is difficult and often subjective, and the virtual nature adds another level of complexity. For the employee being evaluated, other variables present in the virtual form (lack of physical presence, absence of organizational relationships, potential hidden agendas of superiors from corporate partners) can create anxiety and hostility.

Virtual organizations present employees with conflicting organizational demands, beyond issues of loyalty discussed above. Virtual organizations' demands for speed and customization call for teamwork and interdisciplinary cooperation among the organizations' employees. Such demands are difficult in any environment and may be exacerbated in virtual environments with minimal physical and organizational proximity. Employees of virtual organizations may need to take actions beyond those necessary in traditional organizations to achieve the same end results. Beyond the extra effort, this also may place new stresses on employees operating in already resource-scarce environments.

Clancy (1994) says that the virtual organizational form suggests changes in the concept of 'work' and the nature of 'teamwork'. He argues that to optimize the overall effort, a virtual enterprise's managers may view work processes as discrete packages to be allocated to individuals. Doing this optimizes the resources available to the organization, especially in light of underlying demands for timeliness and customization. Beyond questions of allocating these 'packages' are questions relating this view of work to the need for teamwork and cross-functional integration of effort. This particularly is true for telecommuting in virtual work environments.

Thus employees of virtual organizations are pulled in many directions. They must work fast and pay attention to the detail necessary to deliver virtual products; they must work in teams with people not only from functions other than their own, but often from other companies who may be their competitors in other environments; they must be independent and perform with less managerial control that would be the case in a vertically integrated corporation; and if Clancy is right, they must perform this inherently integrative task in discrete work packets. Finally, these same employees may be involved in multiple simultaneous virtual endeavors that add new dimensions to an already complex problem. Therefore, as shown in Figure 4.3, there are several styles of communication between the different parties involved.

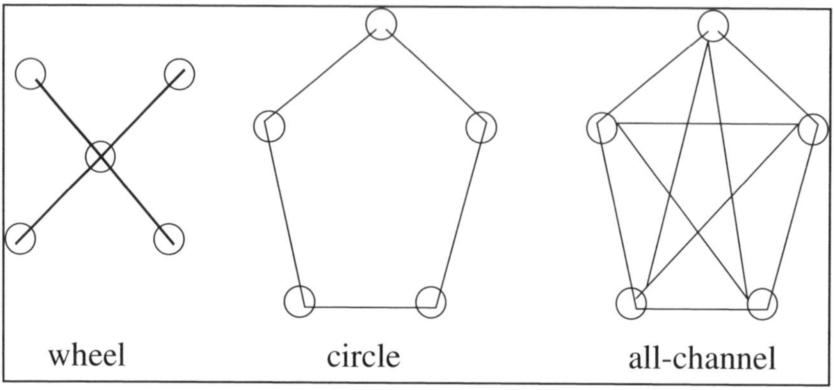

Figure 4.3. Styles of communication (Rada, 1991)

One group of employees in the traditional organizational world facing similar stresses and strains is consultants. Engagements may be thought of as virtual projects, here today and gone tomorrow. The consultants may work with competitors on some projects and may face joint loyalties, both to the client and to their own company. They must work on teams but also may work according to predetermined work ‘packets’, especially on engagements where the work is well defined. Although we will not pursue this analogy here, examining the culture of management consulting and its organizational implications may suggest directions for further examining how the virtual organization affects employees in virtual ventures.

Technology is the final dimension affecting employees of virtual organizations. As discussed above, information technology that increasingly will be Internet-based is the prime facilitator of virtual enterprises, especially in the global arena. Employees must be familiar with the computer and telecommunications technologies and be able to integrate these seamlessly into their daily work. Beyond familiarity with the technologies, virtual organization employees must be able to use the technologies as a platform to add value to their efforts. While technology makes available information to perform many functions, how employees use that information determines the success or failure of the venture. Information must be elevated to knowledge for virtual enterprises to succeed.

Generally, employees in virtual organizations are under less managerial control because a flattening of the managerial hierarchy is a raison d’être of the virtual organization. This means the employee has more responsibility and must make more decisions. This may place new demands for more independent employees than those required in hierarchically organized companies. Again to use the consulting analogy, employees of virtual organizations are engagement managers and are generally on their own, managing their efforts, yet reflecting the values and interests of their parent organization.

4.2.9 Steps to Increase Effectiveness

For the organizational endeavor to succeed, organizations that enter into virtual alliances must take various steps that preserve their interests, facilitate achieving objectives, and drawing out the most from the organization. Five key actions are:

1. *Enter into virtual alliances only when such alliances increase organizational capabilities.* – Organizations should remember that virtual alliances are a means to achieving overall organizational objectives. Virtual alliances make sense when the environment indicates entering into such alliances will give the organization new capabilities that are greater than those it would have under other organizational structures. However, when control is paramount the organization either should forgo the alliance, or should ensure that it will be the controlling partner. As Chesbrough and Teese suggest, virtual organizations exhibiting staying power remain at the center of their network.
2. *Maintain core competencies, particularly regarding technologies.* – Virtual alliances present an ongoing risk of permanently losing core competencies. This is particularly true when the firm enters the alliance to buttress a weak technological posture or to leverage another firm's capabilities to get to the next technological level faster that would normally be possible. Organizations should enter into alliances with eyes open to ensure that transitory advantages do not result in long-term atrophy.
3. *Identify changing demands on employees and institute ongoing education, training and employee development programs.* – Employee education, training and development are important for any organization but are even more crucial in virtual environments where technical skills, knowledge, and ongoing development are critical to organizational success. This not only ensures that employees maintain and develop their skill sets, but ensures that employees represent the parent organization and maintain operational or strategic control.
4. *Maintain an evergreen technology platform and continuously improve how information is used.* – Analyzing and acting on information is a key

enabler in a virtual organization and the employees of the organization must be current on the uses of information technology. Maintaining the platform is important because the platform makes possible two defining characteristics of the virtual organization: speed and flexibility.

5. *Focus on values and trust throughout the organization.* – Employees of organizations in virtual alliances are representatives of those organizations and, by the nature of the alliance, often work under minimal managerial control. To be effective they must have internalized the values of the parent organization. Moreover, they must be honest and trustworthy because in virtual organizations trust is necessary.

Given the changing cultural and corporate environment, the forces that lead to virtual organizations forming and which make them an effective organizational form will increase. Although the virtual world is different, the organizations that profit from virtual alliances will be those to understand the new terrain and act intelligently to cope with the new environment's realities.

4.3 Virtual Organizations and the Law

The title of this section is a bit of a misnomer. Indeed, for the law, virtual organizations do not, or hardly, exist. Most jurisdictions will hold that a *de facto* organization has no rights or obligations of its own, but is nothing but the reflection of its individual membership, each separately responsible in terms of obligations, and possibly, albeit very tentatively in most cases, having individual rights. Save for certain anti-racketeering and (tax) fraud statutes and for competition policy, virtual organizations have seldom been the subject of legal scrutiny.

Still, in the real world of virtual organizations, legal issues abound. These encounters with law are what is described in this section. For the sake of clarity, issues are grouped in four main sections. In none of these descriptions, reference is made exclusively to any specific national law. Instead, the student is merely made aware of legal issues that orbit the concept of virtual organizations. What remains is a collection of legal issues that will need to be managed.

4.3.1 The Concept of Undertaking

An enterprise is variously defined as a business, a project or an undertaking. The latter term may be helpful in our search for what a virtual organizations might constitute, if anything at all, in law.

In its competition policy provisions, particularly article 81(1) EC Treaty (formerly article 85(1) EC), the Treaty makes a reference to *undertakings*, but does not provide for a definition. In *Polypropylene*, the European Commission held that the term was not confined to those entities that possessed legal personality, but covered every entity engaged in commercial activity (Dec. 86/398, [1986] OJ L230/1, [1988] 4 CMLR 347, at 402). The European Court of Justice held that the term covers any entity engaged in economic activity regardless of its legal status and the way in which it is financed (Case C-41/90, *Höfner and Elser v. Macroton GmbH* [1991] ECR I-1979, [1993] 4 CMLR 306; Case C-244/94, *Fédération Française des Sociétés d'Assurance v. Ministère de l'Agriculture et de la Pêche* [1996] 4 CMLR 536; Cases IV/33.126 and IV/33.322, *Cement Cartel* [1995] 4 CMLR 327). So the term 'undertaking' may encompass public or private corporations, co-operatives, partnerships, trade associations, individuals, and any combination thereof. In effect, the term may even be used to describe two legally separate units, e.g. a parent company and its subsidiary, as one economic unit (see e.g. Case 22/71, *Béguelin Import v. GL Import-Export* [1971] ECR 949, [1972] CMLR 81; Dec. 89/113, *Racal Group Services* [1989] OJ L43/27, [1990] 4 CMLR 627; Dec. 91/50, *NV IGMO v. Ijsselcentrale* [1991] OJ L28/32, [1992] 5 CMLR 154).

If one attempts to define a virtual organization legally, one may therefore refer back to the term 'undertaking' as used in European competition law, albeit with the proviso that a virtual organization might have a purely cultural or other, entirely non-economic goal and activities.

4.3.2 The Issue of Applicable Law and Jurisdiction: Contracts

(a) Any organization needs a home base. Incorporated entities have one by virtue of their incorporation in a certain jurisdiction. Virtual organizations may assign one to themselves.

Contracts make up a virtual organization, be they written, oral or implied. In the case of written agreements, one has to see what has been stated as regards applicable law. If an express provision has been made (e.g. "The law applicable to the interpretation and execution of this agreement is the law of the Kingdom of The Netherlands"), then that law will govern interpretation and execution of an agreement.

(b) Applicable law needs to be distinguished from jurisdiction. The jurisdictional issue deals with the tribunal, which will hear and settle disputes, not with applicable law. It makes sense to ensure that if a certain national law is chosen, the courts in that country are stipulated to be the ones that will hear any dispute arising pursuant to the provisions of the agreement (it is often included in a jurisdiction clause that such dispute settlement forum is also competent to hear all requests for provisional measures). But it is not an absolute requirement that applicable law and dispute settlement forum must be the same, and there are instances of a tribunal dealing with the law of another country. One caution should be given: there are also instances in which, in such a case, the tribunal set aside a stipulated law or part thereof, and substituted its own. This may be for reasons, e.g. of 'public order', a notion arising from French administrative law and adopted throughout continental Europe and in the European contentieux (see e.g. Conseil d'Etat, *Minister of the Interior v. Cohn Bendit*, [1980] 1 CMLR 543) or public morality.

(c) An arbitration clause may be an attractive alternative to a jurisdictional clause referring to a national court. While ad hoc clauses are possible, it may be more prudent to avail oneself of the services of an arbitration organization, either national or international. In the latter case, it is worthwhile to refer to the International Chamber of Commerce's arbitration rules (see ICC Publication N° 581, International Court of Arbitration, Rules of Arbitration and Rules of Conciliation, both in force as from 1 January 1998; on the international plane, there are also other sets of rules, e.g. the UNCITRAL model). The ICC's standard arbitration clause reads as follows: "All disputes arising out or in connection with the present contract shall be finally settled under the Rules of Arbitration of the International Chamber of Commerce by one or more arbitrators appointed in accordance with the said Rules."

The clause brings out some of the features of arbitration: the arbitral sentence is final, there is no appeal but there is, in case of need for enforcement, an exequatur – i.e. ratification – procedure needed, given that the dispute settlement is private and that one has to rely on public authority courts for enforcement, hence the 'ratification' by such courts.

One must stipulate whether one or three arbiters shall decide the matter. In the case of a single arbiter, the parties must agree, or, in case of disagreement, the arbitral organization will decide. In the case of three arbiters, each party chooses one and they jointly choose their presiding arbiter. The advantage of the choice of arbiter is not that one seeks a partisan judge – s/he is not – but that one ensures the professional competence of such dispute settler as regards the matter to be judged upon.

The place of arbitration is important enough to be stipulated as it usually determines, at least in principle, the procedural rules to be followed, although arbiters, often from other jurisdictions, may adapt these to suit their particular needs or equity.

(d) In case no law is explicitly made applicable, issues arise as to what law will govern the interpretation and execution of the contract, i.e., each jurisdiction deals differently with conflicts of law, and the first question is, which of such laws shall apply. The answer is to be found in the law on the conflicts of law. Suffice it to say here that not stipulating applicable law in a contract may be fatal for business and partners alike in case of a dispute, as one may spend considerable time and money finding out through various courts what law shall apply, before one arrives at the substantive elements of the dispute at hand. The same is true of applicable law clauses which state problematic choices of law (e.g. "the law of the agreement is that of the defendant party") or choose a law that does not exist (e.g. the law of the United Kingdom, whereas it should be either the law of England and Wales, of Scotland or of Northern Ireland).

Contracts that cover the same or similar events or occurrences should not be covered by different stipulations regarding applicable law and/or jurisdiction.

4.3.3 The Issue of Applicable Law and Jurisdiction: No Written Contracts

In case a virtual organization, rather foolishly, relies on oral agreements only, the above statement on the law of conflicts of law governing applicable law and jurisdiction on the relationship would 'settle' any problems of interpretation and execution of the relationship.

4.3.4 Agency and Distributorship; Employment

The relationship between parties in a virtual organization may, depending on jurisdiction, be qualified as an agency or distributorship relationship, or as employment. Such qualification may have serious results, particularly as regards termination indemnities that may be due at an ending of the relationship by the party deemed to be principal or distribution provider or employer. In addition, there are social security and tax consequences if the relationship is deemed to be one of employment. Care should therefore be taken to stipulate the exclusion of such qualification; at the same time, it should be realized that such stipulation may not be effective if the actual conduct qualifies the relationship as one of agency, distributorship or employment.

4.3.5 Tax Consequences

In principle, all members or elements of a virtual organization will be taxed at the place deemed to be their permanent residence. Insofar as issues of double taxation arise, e.g. as regards the payment to other members of dividends, interest or royalties, reference should be made to avoidance of double taxation treaties. Presently, most of these treaties follow the OECD Model Tax Convention on Income and Capital (see Philip Baker, *Double Taxation Conventions, A Manual on the OECD Model Tax Convention on Income and Capital*, 3rd edition, Sweet & Maxwell, London (loose-leaf)). Withholding taxes are different, per set of treaties and per country policies. Mark in this respect, for example, the situation of The Netherlands, which favors zero withholding and, hence, is often used as a pass-through country for dividends, interest or royalties.

Value-added tax (VAT) on services rendered from one element or member of a virtual organization should not be forgotten. Although VAT charged to non-residents may be recovered by, or for, such non-residents, this may take time, e.g. from 6 to 18 months. Hence the practice of stipulating that certain payments be made net and exclusive of any taxes, meaning that the debtor has to gross up the payment to take care of withholding taxes and VAT.

If virtual organizations have elements or members that are not part of the EU or its customs zone, the issue of customs duties may arise if imports are made.

It should be recalled that certain parts of EU countries are not part of the EU, prominently the Channel Islands and the Isle of Man as well as Gibraltar.

4.3.6 Accounting Law

In accounting law, as in all other areas of law concerning virtual organizations, the first question remains which law and jurisdiction shall be deemed applicable. In this regard, one should recall the difference in treatment awarded to intellectual capital by different accounting laws, either because there are provisions at hand (in Scandinavia) or because there is flexibility beyond current International Accounting Standards (IAS) (e.g. in Gibraltar).

4.3.7 Intellectual Property Rights

Beyond the issue of which law will govern intellectual property (IP) and which jurisdiction shall settle disputes, there arise several issues as to IP ownership. The first one concerns ownership of IP. In this regard, it may be necessary to enter into suitable arrangements so as to link up beneficial ownership with legal ownership. Indeed, it may be that the legal holder of a patent or trademark, or a copyright, database or design, may be only an owner of record, but not the economic owner. In such cases, licenses will need to be entered into so as to ensure that economic, beneficial owners may use and develop the IP. Also, in an attempt to ward off obvious problems in the case of a bankruptcy of the legal owner, rights of first refusal or other forms of attempted recovery of IP may have to be inserted into suitable arrangements. Whether such attempts withstand the applicable bankruptcy law is better opined on before one signs off.

The second issue concerns IP maintenance, particularly if patents are at stake and the cost of maintenance is, hence, high. However, effective trademark protection, by virtue of the possible sheer number of marks to be maintained in manifold jurisdictions, may also pose a problem.

An obvious issue is the division of royalties: specific contractual arrangements will need to be entered into.

4.3.8 Who Represents a Virtual Organization?

Corporations have a structure that stipulates representation towards third parties, but also towards shareholders. Certain organs or positions are mandated to speak for, or on behalf of a corporation. The law of corporations of different countries will spell out what is, and is not, allowed in this regard.

In a virtual organization, that framework is lacking. It may be filled in by contractual arrangements between parties or elements, but these arrangements are not necessarily brought to the attention of, or executable against, third parties. Third parties may judge by appearance. If someone appears to be managing the whole, then s/he may be liable for that appearance. As between parties, that appearance may be qualified as a form of mandate, or as a form of preservation of interests, or as a form of unregistered trusteeship.

If a party managing the whole or specific tasks for the virtual organization misrepresents, or goes beyond internally arranged mandates, and appears to be representing the virtual organization, then all members or elements of that organization may be liable for the appearance created.

The remedy is not an easy one: it means that suitable disclaimers have to be drawn up and attached to practically all communications with the world outside of the virtual organization.

4.4 Prioritization of Needs: Individual, Group or Corporation

The Mass Privatization enterprise (Carter, 2000) is a virtual organization in which each individual owns the specific work performed. People partnered in self-directed teams, teamnets (team-networks) and business units form entire global organizations. They operate in internal supplier/customer chains and clusters, leading to end-user customers. Information technology, the Internet and the incoming Information Superhighway connect partners. Partners and teamnets are compensated by their immediate customers by cash flows in the opposite direction of workflow. There are no managers, salaries or employees. It is a system where passionate and artful Mass Customization replaces passionless and de-humanizing mass production. What we are speaking of with Mass Privatization is a true collaborative free market, enabled by people interconnected through advanced information technology. It is a system with the free and fluid flow of work, ideas, knowledge and trade between individuals, a system of synergy, synthesis and interdependence. Because the individual owns the specific work performed it is 'private work' and because the masses of people in large global organizations are private workers the system is called "Mass Privatization".

With the synthesis of whole work, each owning individual operates a whole business, seeing the entire business process – a quantum worldview. These whole businesses are synthesized together to form self-organizing teams and the teams synthesize to form teamnets, business units and entire organizations or communities.

Is this really the wave of the future? Very much like the forecasted demise of mainframes, COBOL, and tape drives, the hierarchical organization will also continue to co-exist with the newer organizational structures of the 21st century and beyond.

4.4.1 The Role of Trust for the Individual and the Virtual Organization

But what if the role of the individual does not correspond with the direction of the organization? One of the challenges with virtual organizations is managing the needs of the individual, the group and the organization in tandem. Setting expectations, understanding that the base unit of an organization is an individual, and having their needs being met as part of the strategy, is key.

Trust is the heart of the matter (Handy, 1995). Handy stated: "If we are to enjoy the efficiencies and other benefits of the virtual organization, we will have to rediscover how to run organizations based more on trust than on control. Virtuality requires trust to make it work: Technology on its own is not enough." That seems obvious, yet most traditional organizations are arranged on the assumption that people cannot be trusted or relied on, even in the smallest things. Oversight systems are set up to prevent anyone from doing the wrong thing, whether by accident or design.

Writ large, that sort of attitude creates a paraphernalia of systems, checkers, and checkers checking checkers – expensive and deadening. Some commentators have argued that audit mania (the urge to have some independent inspection) is a virus infecting our society. It exists, they suggest, because we no longer trust people to act for anything but their own short-term interests. That attitude becomes a self-fulfilling prophecy (Handy, 1995).

Trust and fear both explain how groups of people who ought to be in partnership with each other, and who want to be in partnership with each other, end up bitterly opposed. It applies to teams working across functions, joint ventures between organizations, union–management battles, suppliers and manufacturers, family disputes, and even civil wars (Senge, 1994, p. 145).

Trust is not blind. It is unwise to trust people whom you do not know well, whom you have not observed in action over time, and who are not committed to the same goals. In practice, it is hard to know more than 50 people that well. Those 50 can each, in turn, know another 50, and so on. Large organizations are not therefore incompatible with the principle of trust, but they have to be made up of relatively constant, smaller groupings. The idea that people should move around as much and as fast as possible in order to get more exposure and more experience – what the Japanese call the horizontal fast-track – can mean that there is no time to learn to trust anyone and, in the end, no point, because the organization starts to replace trust with systems of control.

But control is then after the event, when the results are assessed. It is not a matter of granting permission before the event. Freedom within boundaries works best, however, when the work unit is self-contained, having the capability within it to solve its own problems. Trust-based organizations are, as a result, re-engineering their work, pulling back from the old reductionist models of organization, in which everything was divided into its component parts or functions. At first sight, the new holistic designs for the units of the organization look more expensive because they duplicate functions and do not necessarily replicate each other. The energy and effectiveness released by the freedom within boundaries more than compensates, however.

An organizational architecture made up of relatively independent and constant groupings pushes the organization toward the sort of federal structure that is becoming more common everywhere. A necessary condition of constancy, however, is an ability to change: if one set of people cannot be exchanged for another set when circumstances alter, then the first set must adapt or die. The constant groups must always be flexible enough to change when times and customers demand it. They must also keep themselves abreast of change, forever exploring new options and new technologies. They must create a real learning culture. The choice of people for these groups is therefore crucial. Every individual has to be capable of self-renewal. Recruitment and placement become key, along with the choice of group leaders. Such topics will require the serious attention of senior management. They should not be delegated to a lower echelon of human resources.

One example of changing the dynamic in individual management came from a client of mine in the UK. This PR firm is based in London, and had a hard time maintaining senior account managers because of their location and the needs of the mainly female 30-something staff for childcare, transport and other lifestyle challenges. The firm decided to install a flexi-working program for a certain level of staff member (senior account manager and upwards), in order to provide them both the level of flexibility and level of responsibility to do their job productively in the field. The big issue, addressed by senior management, HR, and the computer help desk, is finding ways to manage someone that you do not see. The management had to put in place initiatives to push managers to create space in the diary to proactively manage these staff by conference calls, written activity logs, and other mechanisms that added value, not created administrative busy work.

The upside is that the headcount stayed stable, and the retention rate shot up as they only lost two staff, not ten as in the previous year. The downside is that the business, due to the economy, did not keep the level of business development at a point where they could expand the program.

By putting formal measures in place, expectations were set and trust was established in that the employee knew what was expected in terms of productivity, and was given the responsibility to make it happen. As the economy changes more towards a knowledge-service economy, away from a physical production economy, the intangible production of intellectual capital will make it more challenging to set the parameters of productivity for a knowledge worker in a virtual organization. We still feel the need to have things we can count and therefore control, such as number of sales calls for revenue generation, number of calls taken for service workers, number of people seen for customer satisfaction, etc. Employers also find the (legal) need to have metrics to promote or give raises, and part of that is metrics on productivity. Creating ways to enable workers in a virtual organization to be productive, yet virtual from their management, will force HR to create new frameworks to view employee functions.

In 1995, Professor Christian Scholz (University of Saarbrücken) presented in the DGFP journal for HR professionals his specific vision of a virtual HR-department. It was designed by transforming the concept of virtual organization known from management theory to Human Resources Management. Although the discussion was controversial in the beginning and drew a lot of criticism, the basic idea of the virtual HR-department is meanwhile accepted as an option for HR organization by academics and practitioners. The virtual HR department is (1) a decentralized network of HR core competencies which are (2) integrated by 'soft' mechanisms like co-destiny or corporate culture and (3) supported by multimedia technology.

What are the opportunities and limits of virtual management? The more decentralized a company operates, the greater the challenges facing human resource work and executives. Employees in different companies and countries must be motivated; work processes must be coordinated worldwide. Professor Ewald Scherm and Stefan Süß (Fernuniversität Hagen) consider this challenge a "management paradox" of modern, decentralized, and spatially spread out organization structures. Can modern information and communication technology help to create the required closeness to the employees? The authors believe that human resource management by e-mail and through videoconferencing cannot replace management in person by competent superiors.

Teams that can bridge the distance gap will win a clear competitive advantage – travelling less but with greater impact during each visit, backed up with regular videoconferencing, shared space technologies, chat, e-mail, telephone conference calls and other digital tools. And forget old-style video-links in boardrooms. Soon video-links will start as spontaneously as a telephone call.

Human resources, information technology, corporate real estate – all these areas need to think together about how teams of tomorrow can operate in the most efficient and human-sensitive way.

4.5 Case Study: Grid Computing via SURFnet

The growing popularity of the Internet along with the availability of powerful computers and high-speed networks as low-cost commodity components are changing the way we do computing. These new technologies enable the clustering of a wide variety of geographically distributed resources, such as supercomputers, storage systems, data sources, and special devices and services, that can then be used as a unified resource. This new paradigm is popularly terms as "Grid" computing. The Grid is analogous to the electrical power grid and aims to couple distributed resources and offer consistent and inexpensive access to resources irrespective of their physical location.

Grid computing can be seen as the emerging enabling technology for facilitating multi-institutional and multi-disciplinary collaborations worldwide.

In the Netherlands, SURF is the organization of collaborating universities and academic institutions that is involved in discussions and planning on infrastructure and other IT matters. Maintaining and developing the actual research network itself is a separate organization called SURFnet.

The SURF Foundation (Stichting SURF), the parent organization, is the most important Dutch cooperative organization for institutions for higher education and research in the field of network services and information and communication technology. Stichting SURF has two subsidiaries, which join forces in specific areas:

- SURFdiensten bv (SURF Services). SURFdiensten grants institutions for higher education and research SURF licenses for a wide range of ICT products, such as software and hardware, at very favorable conditions.
- SURFnet operates and innovates the national research network, to which two hundred institutions in higher education and research in the Netherlands are connected. To remain in the lead, SURFnet puts in a sustained effort to improve the infrastructure and to develop new applications to give users faster and better access to new Internet services.

The SURFnet network enables its users to communicate with other network users and to consult the Internet from their office or their home PC. SURFnet provides rapid and reliable connections to educational institutions and research centers abroad using advanced technologies and high-quality infrastructure.

SURFnet is one of the partners in the GigaPort national project that aims to develop the Next Generation Internet in the Netherlands. The GigaPort project consists of two parts, GigaPort Network and GigaPort Applications. SURFnet is responsible for the network part.

The physical SURFnet network consists of cables that are linked together by various switches and routers. Communication over the network is made possible by providing several protocols such as TCP/IP. This SURFnet network connects its member institutions' local networks to one another and enables member institutions to contact national and international networks that like SURFnet are part of the Internet.

4.5.1 Extension of SURFnet5

SURFnet started extending the number of PoPs in the SURFnet5 network at the end of 2001. Using GigaPort funds, the fifteen current PoPs are being extended with ten additional PoPs. The aim is to increase the density of SURFnet5, reducing the physical distance from the institutions to the network. This makes the rollout of fiber-optics over the last meters from the institutions to SURFnet5 more cost-efficient. The ten additional connection points are connected to the fifteen larger PoPs over two separate lines.

The infrastructure SURFnet uses for this is managed dark fiber. This means that managed optical fiber is delivered, to which SURFnet itself connects active equipment. An important advantage is that no bandwidth is purchased, but the choice of equipment deployed by SURFnet determines the bandwidth. The institutions involved in the different projects are connected at a capacity of 1 Gbit/s, which can be extended later to 10 Gbit/s.

In February 2002 a contract was concluded with BT Ignite for the realization of the PoPs in Alkmaar, Arnhem, Breda, Den Bosch, Deventer and Haarlem. At the same time two institutions in Dordrecht and Nieuwegein will be included in this rollout. In April a contract was signed with BT Ignite for single routes between Maastricht–Heerlen and Groningen–Leeuwarden; contracts are being negotiated for the complementary routes with Essent and KPN, respectively.

In July 2002 contracts were also concluded for the delivery of managed dark fiber for the duration of fifteen years with the following suppliers:

- Global Crossing: for the link Amsterdam–Dwingeloo, which will give the ASTRON observatory a direct multi-gigabit connection to the SURFnet5 PoP in Amsterdam;
- Eurofiber: for a ring infrastructure in Rotterdam, the link Rotterdam–Delft and the link Leiden–Amsterdam. This will give three polytechnics, a research center and a publisher of scientific works a connection at a gigabit level to the SURFnet network;
- Volker Stevin Telecom Infra (VSTI): for a ring infrastructure in Den Haag, which will provide eight organizations in Den Haag and surroundings (polytechnics, research centers and a library) a connection at a gigabit level with the SURFnet network;
- Telecom Utrecht: for a ring infrastructure in the city of Utrecht and for a ring between Houten and Utrecht which will provide three institutions a connection to SURFnet at a gigabit speed.

In April 2003 contracts were concluded for two additions to the existing network. Extra managed dark fiber connects the Province of Drenthe to the SURFnet5 network and a separate network is being built to conduct tests in order to make technical innovation possible without influencing regular network traffic.

SURFnet has also realized an Internet interconnection point to stimulate the technology of fully optical networks. It is used for research purposes only. This experimental Internet interconnection point is hosted by SARA in Amsterdam and is called NetherLight. Between NetherLight and StarLight the T-Systems multi-gigabit/s lambda connection is used. Also a connection of 10 Gbit/s was established by Global Crossing with CERN, the European Organization for Nuclear Research in Geneva.

The initiative for NetherLight and its unique lambda connection emerged from the view that there is a technological and economic boundary to the development of ever larger routers to reach ever higher speeds. SURFnet has therefore developed ideas to realize transport over the Internet in a different manner, in collaboration with the University of Illinois and the International Center for Advanced Internet Research in Chicago, and the Canadian research network organization CANARIE. Research networks and institutions in the Netherlands and abroad can also link their lambdas to NetherLight to research models and technologies for later generations of optical routers.

Questions:
1. SURFnet is used in an academic environment, supported by the Dutch government. What challenges might exist in commercial environments, where the financing of technology does not come from one main source (e.g. a government)? What about approaches to choices in network standards with commercial firms?
2. Discuss how interoperability and standards play a role in how different universities (University of Illinois, CANARIE, etc.) are able to share information across networks such as these.
3. On a shared network such as this, security questions arise. Who should have access to what? How secure should each service be? How much effort should one university willing to put into securing a certain part of their own infrastructure?

4.6 Key terms

Encryption: Encryption is the conversion of data into a form, called a ciphertext, that cannot be easily understood by unauthorized people. Decryption is the process of converting encrypted data back into its original form, so it can be understood.

Group development: In the context of this chapter, this means the evolution of behaviors and communications that reflect group norms.

Source validation: From a security standpoint, this is filtration to determine if the source is legitimate or not. This may be driven by having centralized systems, nice for ease management and scalability, but everything can become a trust issue and a single point of failure or source of problems.

4.7 Review Questions

1. How do the security issues of traditional organization compare to a virtual organization?
2. How does technology help or hinder management of a virtual organization?
3. What role does technology play in organizational effectiveness, particularly in virtual alliances?
4. Explain the concept of undertaking, in terms of legal definition of a business.
5. Discuss how priorities for an organization may not correspond with the individual.

Chapter 5

PEOPLE AND TECHNOLOGY

Introduction

The necessary trends of agility, mass-customization, globalization of markets and supply sources and the increasing demand for extended products by consumers, are shifting the competitive focus to complex and rapidly changing virtual organizations. The primary contribution of this chapter is to discuss the virtual organization and how it provides dynamism to the traditional operational mechanisms.

Most contributions in recent IS literature deal with the structure of virtual organizations. Little emphasis is put on the process of formation and operation of virtual organizations. In combining both structure and process, we can not only understand and comment on the structure and process of virtual organizations, but we can also explain, by using a process perspective, how the structure of a virtual organization comes about.

Learning Objectives of the Chapter

When you have completed this chapter, you should be able to:

- Discuss the changing role of technology in product development
- Elaborate on how technology enables the supply chain, both in terms of production and information flows
- Explain how the Internet and network technologies have streamlined the procurement process.

5.1 Product Development and Customization via Virtual Technology

Virtual product development management makes testing the consequences of 'what if?' scenarios easy and fast. Changes can be updated and tracked to help developers maximize their efforts, while preventing changes made in one stage of development from creating problems in another. And all of this is done without the expense of physical prototypes.

Product lifecycle management (PLM) has been a long-standing area of activity of collaboration between different contributors to the final product. Non-real-time collaboration – also known as 'contextual' collaboration – is how the majority of work gets done. As anyone who ever participated in a cross-functional design team knows, having everyone in the same room at the same time arguing over how to design a product leads to sub-optimized designs, also known as the lowest common denominator effect. Great design minds can tag-team back and forth, each building on the others' ideas, but they generally can't work by committee.

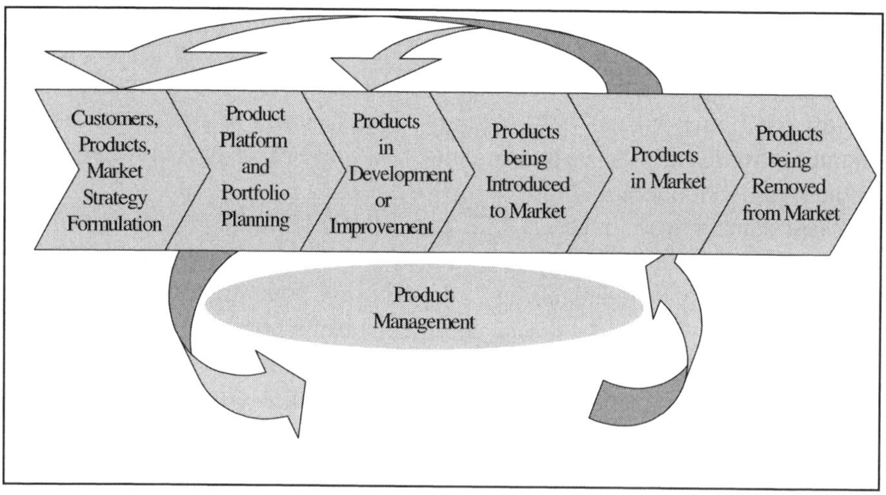

Figure 5.1. Product Lifecycle Management

What is important is to eliminate the inefficiencies that time, distance and differing professional disciplines introduce to the process. The ideal is to let each team member accomplish his or her work *as if* the entire team were assembled behind them at all times, ready to answer questions and provide context as each decision is made. In this way, collectively, the team, as shown in Figure 5.1, arrives at the optimal combination of function, form, cost, quality and performance while efficiently accommodating different schedules and work styles.

Virtual product development, via e-collaboration, requires complex connections among a multitude of existing systems and sophisticated middleware to translate data from one system to another in a way that will make sense to the user based on his or her job function. That means e-collaboration is not just an application dropped on top of existing systems – it begins with the foundation that defines the fundamental interactions of those systems. Information will not flow and facilitate e-collaboration unless it is attached to a good foundation of tightly linked enterprise systems.

A good foundation accommodates the fact that different types of collaboration occur at different points of time among a multitude of job functions – even long after a product has left the factory and is being supported in the field. Throughout the product development lifecycle, customer requirements are determined, product portfolios are planned and developed, individual activities are executed, products are configured and optimized, suppliers are integrated into the process, designs are created and reviewed and logistics and distribution are coordinated. In the process, a multitude of systems is accessed, including CRM, portfolio management, conceptual design, detailed design, SCM, PDM, ERP and service and support.

Some of these activities happen in real-time, and tools like virtual meeting rooms, Web-enabled markup and electronic whiteboarding are valuable in such settings. But e-collaboration actually reduces the need for real-time interaction by giving everyone involved not just the information they need, but the context around that information.

With a strong data foundation to support it, e-collaboration finally makes it possible to work asynchronously, reducing the need for meetings by allowing all participants to efficiently exchange product information even when it must be accessed, utilized and *understood* by large numbers of people and companies, many of whom have never interfaced before.

Properly architectured (and that is the key point and the real challenge), contextual e-collaboration *ensures that all collaborators have the appropriate access to the correct information in the correct context at the correct time to take the correct actions*. This occurs at all phases of the product development process. The cornerstone is a living data model, which means that data is located in one 'virtual' place, even thought the data physically resides all over the world.

Real-time collaboration can take advantage of e-tools that allow people in different places to evaluate designs using interactive simulation. Digital mockup of the virtual product model allows everyone to reach a full understanding of the product and of how changes affect downstream processes. For the first time, e-collaboration allows product development to be open to the extended organization through Web access to a 'live' product model. Familiar complementary technologies can now be integrated with the underlying system architecture, allowing participants to take advantage of shared conferencing, whiteboarding and markup in new, more meaningful ways. Even after-sales support and maintenance can be integrated into the process, because the virtual product model allows technicians in the field to leverage the original design documents and data context as they service and maintain the product.

5.2 Virtual Manufacturing

Manufacturing companies throughout the world are rapidly changing in order to survive in today's highly competitive market environments. Some examples of coping with changing environments are manufacturing globalization, automated and intelligent manufacturing, virtual manufacturing, and agile manufacturing. The objective of the movement in manufacturing is to improve flexibility, reliability, and productivity, and to achieve competition-based technology development.

From a technological perspective, manufacturing has always been about technical change achieved from the productive use of labor and capital, in the form of plant and equipment.

Conventional machining systems rely heavily on human operators for monitoring the process, taking the appropriate action in the event of a problem, inspecting the quality of the product, controlling the process and material handling (Silvas *et al.*, 2000). However, in recent years, the manufacturing industry has been directed towards automated, untended operation with the goal of achieving better product quality and greater overall productivity and reliability. So, for example, an implementation of an intelligent machining system, which can perform specified machining operations without detailed input from human operators under harsh and unpredictable shop environment, becomes increasingly important.

New advances in computerized modeling, visualization, simulation, and product data management are making virtual manufacturing a viable alternative to traditional product realization/manufacturing.

Driven by the wider availability of low-cost 3D graphics hardware, and advances in Internet technology that make it easier for even complex information to be disseminated from UNIX workstations to desktop PCs, virtual manufacturing is the wave of the future. It will enable companies to reduce design and production costs, ensure product quality, and slash the time needed to go from product concept to production – making it possible to respond instantly to continually changing market and world conditions.

In a manufacturing environment without computers, a designer would draw and draft the components of a product in a detailed ID diagram. In order to verify that the various components and parts would work together, a physical model would have to be built and tested. The results of these tests would be analyzed and modifications would be made by the designer in the original drawings to reflect the asked for enhancements and improvements. The quality of a product would be determined by a manual process, prone to natural human errors and high costs associated with building prototypes, repeated testing, and redesign.

The advent of computer-aided design (CAD) systems has changed all that. CAD, computer-aided manufacturing (CAM), computer-aided engineering (CAE), design for assembly (DFA), design for manufacture (DFM) and visualization and simulation software have helped to bring about significant reductions of time and costs in manufacturing. Computer-integrated manufacturing (CIM), which allows engineers to take information from a CAD system and utilize it in a CAM environment, has provided one model for unifying all of the computer-aided processes involved in manufacturing. CIM technologies allow the use of product data across a spectrum of applications without requiring the recreation, and subsequent loss of valuable information in translation, of that data.

Extended supply chains and extranets, as recent trends in the manufacturing sector, are benefited by virtual manufacturing. User demand for faster, more powerful technologies has shortened product lifecycles dramatically in the last two decades, decreasing manufacturers' opportunity to make profits on new products and forcing them to accommodate multiple product generations in their planning and production cycles. As a result, high-tech companies have increasingly turned to contract manufacturers (CMs) as faster, more cost-effective channels for procuring parts and producing products. These CMs can offer both economies of scale and access to less expensive labor pools as well as specific manufacturing expertise. The result of this outsourcing has been the creation of broad virtual manufacturing networks that often span the globe.

Despite their economic justification, these extended supply chains have created new barriers to productivity because they increase the complexity of communication between participants. Manufacturers and their supply chain partners typically handle communication across the geographically dispersed supply chain using a variety of means: e-mails for regular interaction, faxes for exchanges requiring documentation, or real-time input and phone calls for emergencies. Although there may be some sharing of information systems, the number of participants and their varying business requirements makes widespread installation and integration of a 'single' information system impractical.

The challenge for the manufacturer is that, while each of these enterprises is, theoretically, focused on the same goal – such as delivering a finished PDA to the market – their status as discrete participants in a larger process means they very likely have different operational procedures, communication styles and technical environments. With that in mind, their ability to integrate activities, data and timetables sufficiently to effect the kind of tight communication and action necessary to act as a single unit can be hard to orchestrate.

5.3 Supply Chain Integration

Extended Supply Chain Management applications expand the scope of traditional SCM systems by coordinating multiple suppliers, internal/ external SCM systems, and SMEs (including 75% of manufacturing concerns) to create collaboration and meet global market demand (Fingar, 2000). An extended supply chain management system differs with traditional SCM systems in the extent to which a company can integrate with its suppliers, their suppliers, trading partners, customers and their customers. By sharing information all the way from the point of sale to the inventory levels of suppliers' suppliers, all participants in an extended supply chain system can gain competitive advantage, optimizing performance and profits.

Transactions in the business to business electronic commerce are usually long-lived propositions involving negotiations, commitments, contracts, floating exchange rates, shipping and logistics, tracking, varied payment instruments, exception handling and customer satisfaction. Business transactions have two basic distinguishing characteristics. Firstly, they extend the scope of traditional transaction processing as they may encompass classical transactions, which they combine with non-transactional processes. Secondly, they group both classical transactions as well as non-transactional processes together into a unit of work that reflects the semantics and behavior of their underlying business task. In addition to these basic requirements, business transactions are generally governed by contracts and update accounts and may include the exchange of bills and invoices, and exchange of financial information services. As a consequence, business transactions must provide modeling support and mediate communication, interaction, and coordination among collaborating people and business activities within and between organizations. Business transaction characteristics are better addressed by a process-centered approach to transaction management that supports long-lived concurrent, nested, multi-threaded activities (Leymann and Roller, 1997).

The key is that through electronic collaboration – increased collaboration with traditional suppliers, new SME suppliers, multiple supply chains and customers – all participants can gain breakthrough advantage. The holistic view of the entire supply chain is accompanied by a holistic bottom line for the entire channel. Trading partners can go so far as price indexing rather than negotiated fixed prices in order to equally share gains or losses due to price fluctuations. This dispersion of risk on price is but one benefit to creating a network of supply alliances.

With e-commerce technologies such as JAVA ('write once, run anywhere (WORA)') and XML (the Web's new universal file system), SCM systems of larger players can be extended to the browsers of SMEs, opening up new sources of supply, providing new channel-wide information sharing opportunities. The Internet affords breakthrough cost savings and enables new business opportunities for both big and small suppliers.

The term 'supply grid' is more familiar within the energy industry, with water and electricity supplied by grids of stations and pumping plants. In this case, buyers and sellers create a value network of different-sized partners, allowing risk optimization by creating a network of suitable partners. With the goal of optimizing entire supply grids, success requires 'systems thinking', a business discipline derived from general systems theory. System dynamics helps us understand how things change through time based on the 'systems thinking' approach. Professor Jay W. Forrester (1961) of MIT created system dynamics during the mid-1950s. This discipline evolved from prior work in feedback control systems, and progressively its application was extended to fields other than engineering, such as environmental sciences, social sciences, economics, software development, and enterprise management (Casado, 2002). Systems thinking takes into account internal feedback effects within a system, a concern usually ignored when information from analytic applications is directly used, which can lead us to make 'counterintuitive' decisions (a word Forrester used to describe actions that we believe right to meet a goal, but that have a null or opposite effect).

Most workers involved in supply chain management, however, are not trained to think of optimizing the whole system, just the parts of the system (silos) encompassed by their responsibilities and activities (Fingar, 2000). Optimizing individual silos, however, does not optimize the overall system – these are lessons learned from a decade of business process engineering, only now these lessons must cross company boundaries, and companies need to recognize that their suppliers' costs are ultimately their costs. Those that recognize this are able to overcome the natural barriers to information sharing. Figure 5.2 illustrates the participants and shared business processes of extended supply chain management systems enabled by electronic commerce.

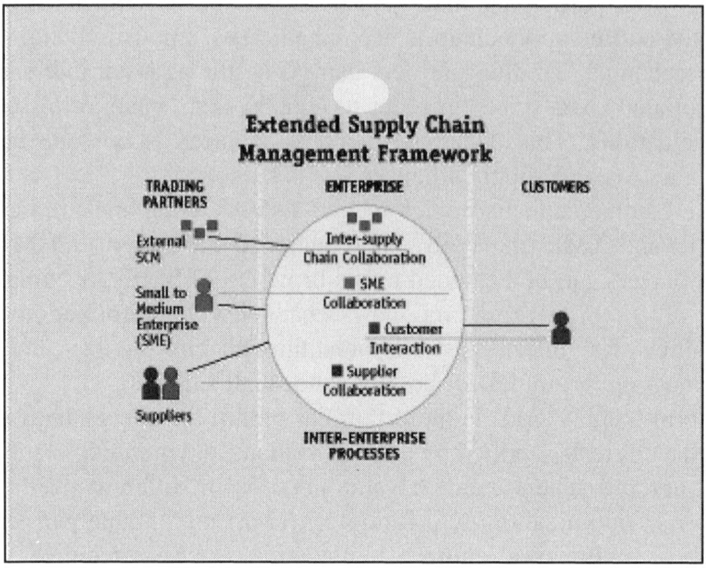

Figure 5.2. Inter-supply chain collaboration (Fingar, 2000)

Multi-divisional companies typically operate multiple supply chain management systems to handle multiple plants and distribution channels. A manufacturer, for example, can configure multiple supply chains to deal with supplier; distribution and customer service channels needed to reach a variety of customers around the globe. Value chains are being made into multiple-path, multiple-node value Webs. An extended SCM system can allow traditional, tightly linked systems to share information across channels and provide new opportunities for optimization across multiple, external supply chains.

In the future, supply chains will function as a real-time business ecosystem. The richness and low cost of the Internet makes it possible to add new collaboration links with existing suppliers – and their suppliers – for forecasting, logistics, replenishment, bidding and ordering. A given supplier may participate in multiple supply chains, and integrating information from them can give the supplier a consolidated information base for planning and operations. Collaborations can be ongoing or ad hoc in response to market events and conditions. Effective contracting for complementary capabilities through a network of suppliers and subcontractors is a characteristic of virtual organizing (Sieber and Griese, 1999).

One interesting point to note is that research has shown companies narrowing down their choices of partners to a few long-term relationships, and participating in supply chain activities like electronic auctions, such as for spot purchasing.

Clemons *et al.* (1993) discussed how, as IT increases information availability and processing capacity, coordination costs, operations risk and opportunism risk are all reduced. The results are reduced need for ownership and more outsourcing due to lower transaction costs. On the other hand, reducing the transaction costs will lead to more *explicit coordination* that generates highly integrated inter-organizational relationships involving significant investment in human relationships and organizational processes. In order to recoup these specific investments in financial settlements, firms will choose to allocate businesses among fewer financial suppliers over a long period of time. In addition, increasing the level of explicit coordination will increase product differentiation, which in turn will increase search costs and thus decrease the benefits of search among a large number of suppliers.

Combining these factors with the need to give firms incentives for making *non-contractible* investments, Clemons *et al.* (1993) concluded that firms would favor developing long-term, value-adding partnerships with a small group of suppliers. This is technologically evidenced through EDI activities, as well as the push for standards in e-markets and e-auctions.

Through a customer self-service business model, fewer customer service personnel are needed as customers gain automated access to the overall supply chain. They can independently browse and price products, configure and order them, look up shipment schedules, and track delivery. The result is customer-driven supply chains and increased customer satisfaction. Internal and external logistics functions will blur and, with a robust supply chain infrastructure, 'spot' markets will appear as companies respond to actual demand data rather than soft forecasts.

5.4 E-Procurement

It has been expected in e-business that purchasing firms would maintain established long-term relationships with preferred suppliers. As a result, private aggregating and negotiating mechanisms within virtual environments are being adopted for large quantity business supply purchases, while public market mechanisms, such as auctions outside of the virtual organization, are more often adopted with spot purchasing when firms face uncertain and high variance demand.

The National Association of Purchasing Management (NAPM) and Forrester Research, Inc. has been tracking online activity for both manufacturing and non-manufacturing organizations. Their third report, published in July 2001, found that nearly 73 percent of organizations use the Internet for indirect purchases, an increase from 71 percent in the previous quarter. During the same period, 54 percent of buyers reported using the Internet to purchase direct materials, an increase from the previous quarter's level of 46 percent. The online buyers reported sending 9.8 percent of their total direct materials order over the Internet.

The procurement process normally consists of several steps, including: selecting product, finding the right vendor, negotiating price, getting approvals, ordering product, receiving product, and paying the invoice. The time, labor, and resources associated with this process cost companies millions of dollars each year. Errors or delays in shipment add to procurement costs, slow down the design process and leave people waiting for products they need to complete their jobs on schedule. Procurement professionals are under tremendous pressure to eliminate errors and reduce these costs.

E-procurement systems accomplish this in several ways. First, they eliminate paperwork by generating electronic purchase orders and routing them instantaneously to the correct person for approval and execution. This increases the purchasing staff's productivity. Second, e-procurement systems compel end-users to purchase from preferred vendors with whom the company has negotiated contracts. Finally, e-procurement systems allow management to track spending with individual suppliers and product categories – giving visibility to problem areas. A billion-dollar corporation can save tens of millions of dollars.

Currently the big names in e-procurement are focusing on automation of requisitioning, approval and ordering processes. But procurement has about 12 other processes that it manages. There are not many software companies focusing on these other processes, but that will change very soon as companies demand more comprehensive global sourcing solutions.

Over time, experts expect technology solutions that:

- Alleviate market fragmentation.
- Allow people to see and manage suppliers across vast geographical spaces.
- Allow multiple companies, with disparate legacy information systems, to link up and move data in real time, at very low cost.
- Allow companies to turn data into information for decision support.
- Create virtual spaces where people can meet, share ideas, make deals, negotiate contracts, manage risks, conduct value analysis and value engineering, and collaborate, in real time, on the design of new products and manufacturing processes.
- Lower cost structures (costs of buying, costs of selling) leading to lower prices without lowering profitability.
- Provide better delivery channels for goods and services.

This shift in emphasis will be driven, in part, by increased buy-side participation in shaping the future of e-procurement. As supply management organizations awake to the possibilities in e-procurement, they are expected to exert more influence on the types of products and services being offered.

Ultimately companies are going to outsource large pieces of their procurement work. There is value in identifying world-class suppliers and understanding the levers that lower costs. E-procurement providers will create huge benefits in this area especially for small and mid-size companies that cannot necessarily develop this expertise on their own.

The complexities and costs of implementing and supporting the necessary technology solutions can quickly dilute the benefits of e-procurement. One of the key technological issues of e-procurement is standards. Integration of supplier data and purchasing details with ERP systems for accounts payable and tax information and CRM for customer data, for example, requires standards in data types, catalogue structure, and other elements of logistics information.

Suppliers have to find a way to capture, manage and deliver the content according to the e-procurement vendor's specifications along with the individual customer's designated commodities and contract pricing. There is the added challenge of taking raw data that resides in internal back end systems and creating clean searchable product descriptions, product attributes, units of measure, and product names. There is also the mandate of supporting multiple coding classifications such as the UNSPSC (United Nations Standard Products and Services Code) or RUS (Requisite Unified Structure) to support drill down as well as internal commodity tracking.

Purchasers want to know the location of their order in the fulfillment process, such as whether the 50 cases of a product have actually shipped. Suppliers need to support real-time access to this product data via the emerging XML standard. And while XML may be the basic standard, each procurement vendor has its own nuances for the same transactions.

While many view e-procurement as new technology, it really amounts to a complete transformation of business processes. Many companies make the mistake of selecting the technology first and then trying to adjust processes to fit the product. If using the system internally is not mandated, buyers will typically pick up the phone and call their favorite supplier, whether under contract or not. Many suppliers have been slow to adopt the move to e-procurement due to a fear of commoditization, insufficient catalog data, and an unwillingness to invest in high technology. Standards are also in a state of flux, with each vendor using its own version of XML, via cXML, xmlCBL, and other versions.

The focus on cost savings is the driving force of e-procurement. The connectivity between businesses and all levels of the supply chain will be greater when cost savings can be seen. But not all business share the same level of business processes, making integration with a different sized supplier all that much more challenging. Global suppliers participating in e-procurement must adapt to issues like language and currency conversions, order processing, and of course the tariffs, customs, and logistics of handling global orders.

According to a 2001 survey by Palmer and Associates (NAPCP, 2001), the five items of greatest concern to the respondents about e-procurement are integration of e-procurement solutions with legacy/ERP information systems, lack of a technology standards, dealing with anonymous vendors, general lack of awareness as to which solutions best meet company needs, and lack of organizational readiness for e-procurement technology. This survey also found that organizations involved in e-procurement perceive the technology to be a greater threat to system security and data integrity.

Across all e-procurement technology models, organizations identify lack of participation by suppliers as a major concern. If buyers 'build it' (an e-procurement infrastructure), it is essential that suppliers come. Therefore data standards and technology integration are crucial issues to e-procurement adoption.

5.5 Case Study: Mach Speed Product Development: Inside the Skunk Works

Acknowledgements to Christopher A. Sawyer, Executive Editor, Automotive Design & Production, Gardner Publications, Inc., Cincinnati, OH.

Of all the organizations established to develop products quickly and creatively, the Lockheed Martin Skunk Works probably is the most famous. But how has this concern, founded in 1943, adapted to 21st-century mission requirements?

Since its creation in 1943, the Skunk Works, now part of Lockheed Martin Aeronautics (Palmdale, California), has grown to three facilities: Burbank, California, Fort Worth, Texas, and Palmdale, California. "Historically," says Gary Ervin, vice president, Advanced Development Programs, "the company's three aeronautics locations competed against one another because they were separate profit and loss centers. But the changing defense picture" – marked by a decrease in both appropriations and programs – "has forced us to rethink the Skunk Works' place in the organization."

That resulted in tearing down the walls between the three locations, as well as those that had built up around the Skunk Works itself. And though the three sites still operate, they have been combined into a single 'virtual' organization under the "Advanced Development Programs" (ADP) banner. Within ADP there are two sub-groups: Advanced Systems Concepts and Advanced Design Center. Ervin explains, "The Advanced Systems Concepts group designs the next-generation bomber, fighter, airlifter (cargo aircraft or tanker), or unmanned vehicle. The Advanced Design Center is full of creative people who look at what future defense needs might be, design systems that can satisfy those requirements, and present them to the various government agencies."

The Skunk Works is doing what it has always done (i.e. develop new aircraft concepts for immediate-need and evolving mission situations). It's just doing it more efficiently.

New capabilities include a Product Improvements and Derivatives (PID) group that gives the Skunk Works responsibility for all improvements to, and derivatives of, existing platforms, and works directly with the group responsible for technology development and integration. "This gives us an entrée into programs, and allows us to apply new technologies to an F-22 fighter program, C-5 cargo plane program, or whatever," says Ervin. "Conversely, if they have requirements for things like a new capability, they present that challenge to us. It's our job to help them satisfy those requirements by providing the necessary technologies."

Sometimes, that technology already existed within the organization, but getting it out into the open was difficult at best because, as Ervin says, "each program created a silo that kept solutions inside the program's walls." The answer was the creation of the Cross-Product Integration (CPI) unit within the ADP organization. Its assignment is to understand the needs of each program, ferret-out existing solutions, and bring them out into the open where they can be shared. "CPI is working very, very well," effuses Ervin. "It has created a 'library' of ideas that has allowed us to get problems solved and answers out to the organization much, much more quickly than ever before." This brings the Skunk Works closer to its original focus of inventing innovative aircraft concepts and sharing its technologies with the rest of the organization, where feasible.

The key to making this complex virtual organization work isn't more time on commercial airliners, says Ervin, it's communication. "My travel time is up," he admits, "but it's not as bad as I thought it would be. Each facility has different capabilities, and folding them into one organization meant creating common procedures, using common tools, and speaking a common language." Now most work is accomplished via Internet meetings, videoconferences, e-mail, and other electronic media.

"We use the same set of electronic databases at all three sites," says Ervin. "And most of the time our suppliers are part of the same database structure. So we send the files back and forth electronically, and the suppliers build the parts and ship them to us without ever having to make prototypes. The concept is the same whether we are dealing with our suppliers or ourselves. Integrated electronic tools are key to opening the lines of communication."

Those tools, however, aren't proprietary. "We use CATIA as a design tool, and that capability was developed with Boeing when we worked together on the YF-22 fighter program," says Ervin. "It made it possible for us to work collaboratively and hurry the process along significantly."

Ervin stated that there are two major things that make them different than others. "First, we look for people with a 'can-do' attitude. People who are free thinkers, creative, and don't let conventional boundaries get in their way. Second, he adds almost off-handedly, "we don't have a standard set of management tools for every situation. We tailor and adapt them to the program. A small, 'black' [covert] program has very different requirements from a large, commercial program," he continues. "We tailor what we do to whatever is appropriate to the program we are working on. It never pays to get lost in the process."

How does this fit with the 14 rules established by Skunk Works founder Clarence L. "Kelly" Johnson (see "Kelly Johnson's 14 Rules") and used on every program from the P-80 Shooting Star through the F-117 Stealth Fighter? "Very well, actually," says Ervin. "Like Kelly, we're firm believers in small focused groups, the need for a program manager with complete control and authority over the program, and empowered individuals who complete a particular task. This maximizes the ability of your team to get the job done as quickly and efficiently as possible, without going completely outside the lines of the organization."

Yet the constant expansion and contraction must have an effect on staffing, especially those empowered, creative types, right? "The Skunk Works grows and shrinks based on what we're doing," Ervin says matter-of-factly. "Between programs we do a lot of R&D, both under contract and internally. So we can move people back into the development side once a program is completed. Or, to take the X-35 Joint Strike Fighter as an example, we send out people who support that program as it moves into production. Then we backfill within the Skunk Works with new people. This helps us stay dynamic and agile on a number of levels, and makes certain this isn't your typical nine-to-five job."

By moving some Skunk Works personnel into the main business, Lockheed Martin has been able to give employees a first-hand look at the way that organization runs. According to Ervin, "Our non-Skunk Works employees have been very impressed by how quickly things can be accomplished. Something breaks, we identify it, and the fix is implemented in a very short time. It's been so successful, that we are looking to roll-out the Advanced Development Program concept beyond the aeronautics division, and into the whole company," he says. "It's amazing what you can do when you give people the wherewithal to go create and perform."

Kelly Johnson's 14 Rules

Named after the mysterious moonshine operation in the "L'il Abner" comic strip, the Skunk Works started small, and worked hard to stay that way. The high-risk nature of its programs were such that success was far from guaranteed, and its small size meant that failure of any one program would not bankrupt Lockheed. For Skunk Works founder Clarence L. "Kelly" Johnson, risk was good for business. And it didn't hurt that it helped create aviation landmarks like the P-80 Shooting Star (America's first production jet fighter), F-104 Starfighter (the world's first Mach 2 aircraft), U-2 (still the highest flying single-engine airplane), SR-71 Blackbird (the fastest, highest flying aircraft ever developed), and F-117 Stealth Fighter (the world's first operational low-observable aircraft).

To minimize the risk as much as possible, while maintaining the greatest agility and creativity possible in a lean team, Johnson established the unit's 14 Basic Operating Rules. They cover everything from program management to compensation, and are relevant for any advanced research unit within a larger organization. The rules, which date back to 1943, are:

1. The program manager must be given practically complete control of every aspect of the program, and report to a division president or higher.
2. Both customer and contractor must have strong but small project offices in order to keep overhead down and communications up.
3. The number of people connected to the project must be severely restricted. Use a small number of good people.
4. Drawing and release systems must be simple, have the flexibility necessary to make changes as needed, and allow the engineers to see how the elements blend together.
5. Reporting requirements must be kept to a minimum, though important work must be thoroughly recorded.
6. There must be a monthly cost review covering not only what has been spent and committed, but also the projected costs to the conclusion of the program.
7. The contractor must be delegated authority, and assume more than normal responsibility to get good vendor bids for subcontracts.
8. Much of the basic inspection responsibility must be put back on the subcontractors and vendors.
9. The contractor must be delegated the authority to test his final product in flight.

10. The specification applying to the hardware must be agreed to in advance of contracting.
11. Funding must be timely. Fixed price R&D contracts are bad business, as are cost and technology sharing.
12. There must be mutual trust between the project organization and contractor, with very close day-to-day cooperation and liaison.
13. Access by outsiders to the project must be strictly controlled by appropriate security measures.
14. Because only a few people will be used in engineering and most other areas, you must provide ways to reward good performance by pay that is not based on the number of personnel supervised.

Exercises:
If Boeing uses the same tools as Lockheed Martin – and has its own Skunk Works in the form of Phantom Works, acquired when Boeing bought McDonnell Douglas – what makes the Skunk Works different from its competition?

5.6 Key Terms

Supply chain: The network of retailers, distributors, transporters, storage facilities and suppliers that participate in the sale, delivery and production of a particular product. The supply chain starts from the origin of the raw material and ends once the product has been discarded or recycled.

Product development: The product evolution, expressed in the developer's language to respond to a customer need. A good development requirement should be (1) stated so that it is directly actionable by engineering, (2) global and does pre-suppose a particular technical solution, and (3) measurable so that it can be ultimately verified. The developer uses the product requirements to guide the design and building of the product.

Product lifecycle management: Product Lifecycle Management (PLM) generally refers to the process of managing all data related to the product over its life cycle. It broadens the concept of product data management (PDM) to address managing the product configuration and the availability of product data into its later lifecycle stages of production, operation, support and disposal and to address managing the product's related process data.

5.7 Review Questions

1. How does the changing role of technology feature in virtual product development?
2. What role does PLM have in integrating information between supplier and producer?
3. Elaborate on how technology enables the supply chain, both in terms of production and information flows. What is the concern of a manufacturer in a virtual organization, both in terms of technology and in terms of organizational processes?
4. Explain how the Internet and network technologies have streamlined the procurement process.
5. How does automation of ordering, for example, impact the other procurement processes?

REFERENCES

Introduction

Saabeel, W. Verduijn, T.M., Hagdorn, L. and Kumer, K. (2002). 'A Model of Virtual Organisation: A Strucutre and Process Perspective', *Electronic Journal of Organizational Virtualness*, Retreived June 2003 from: <http://www.virtual-organization.net/>.

Chapter 1

The American Heritage Dictionary of the English Language, Fourth Edition, Houghton Mifflin Co; ISBN: 0618082301; 4th edition (September 14, 2000).

Bush, V. (1945). 'As we may think'. in Kochen Manfred. *The Growth of Knowledge: Readings on Organization and Retrieval of Information*. New York, NY: Wiley (Reprinted from the *Atlantic Monthly*, 176(1), July 1945, pp. 101-108); 1967: 209-15.

Canter, D., Rivers, R. and Storrs, G. (1985). Characterising user navigation through complex data structures. *Behaviour and Information Technology*, 4, 93-102.

Handy, C. (1995). 'Trust and the Virtual Organization', *Harvard Business Review*, 73 (3): 40-50.

Hardman, L. and Sharratt, B.S. (1989). 'User-Centred Hypertext Design: The Application of HCI Design Principles and Guidelines'. In *HYPERTEXT II: State of the Art*, pages 252-259. 1989.

Harris, M. (1998) 'Rethinking the virtual organization', in: Jackson, P., Van der Wielen, J. (eds.): *Teleworking: International Perspectives – From Telecommuting to the Virtual Organiation,* 74-92, London, UK.

Hewett, T., Baecker, R. Card, S., Carey, T, Gasen, J., Mantei, M., Perlman, G., Strong, G. and Verplank, W. (1992) ACM SIGCHI Curricula for Human-Computer Interaction, Report of the ACM Special Interest Group on Computer-Human Interaction Curriculum Development Group (1992). Retrieved June 2003 from: <http://sigchi.org/cdg/cdg2.html>.

Hodges, M. and Sasnett, R. (1993). *Multimedia Computing*. Reading, MA: Addison-Wesley Publishing Company.

Karpinski, R. (1996). *Beyond HTML*. Berkeley, CA: Osborne McGraw-Hill.

Kim, D. (1993). 'The Link between Individual and Organizational Learning', *Sloan Management Review*, Fall: 37-50.

Large, A. (1996). 'Computer Animation in an Instructional Environment'. *Library and Information Science Research*, 18: 3-23.

Latchem, C., Williamson, J. and Henderson-Lancett, L. eds. (1993). *Interactive Multimedia*. London: Kogan Page Limited.

Law, J. and Callon, M. (1992). 'The Life and Death of an Aircraft: A Network Analysis of Technological Change'. pp. 20-52 in Bijker, Wiebe, and Law, John (eds.) *Shaping Technology / Building Society Studies in Sociotechnological Change*. Cambridge, MA: MIT Press

McAleese, R. (ed.) (1989). *Hypertext: Theory into Practice*. Norwood, NJ: Ablex Publishing Corporation.

McAleese, R. and Green, C. (eds.) (1990). *Hypertext: State of the Art*. Norwood, NJ: Ablex Publishing Corporation.

Nielsen, J. (1990). *Hypertext and Hypermedia*. Boston: Academic Press, Inc.

Nielson, J. (1990). 'The art of navigating through hypertext'. *Communications of the ACM*, 33 (3): 296-310.

Rada, R. (1991). *Hypertext: From text to Expertext*. New York: McGraw-Hill Book Company.

Rouet, J., Levonen, J., Dillon, A. and Spiro, R. (eds.) (1996). *Hypertext and Cognition*. Mahwah, NJ: Lawrence Erlbaum Associates.

Seiter, C. and Negrino, T. (1995). *Macworld Web Essentials*. Foster City, CA: IDG Books Worldwide.

Theise, E. (1995). 'Squealing and Hissing: A gopher client roundup'. In Levine & Baroudi (eds.), *Internet Secrets*. Foster City, CA: IDG Books Worldwide.

Ventura C.A. (1988). 'Why switch from paper to electronic manuals?', Proc. ACM Conf. Document Processing Systems (Santa Fe, NM, 5-9 Dec 1988), pp.111-116.

Chapter 2

Begeman, M. L., and Conklin, J. (1988). 'gIBIS: A hypertext tool for exploratory policy discussion', *ACM Transactions on Office Information Systems*, 6 (4): 303-331.

Davenport, T. (1996). 'Software as Socialware', CIO, March 1, 1996, Retrieved June 2003 from <http://www.cio.com/archive/030196/dave.html>.

DeSantis, G. and Gallupe, R. (1987). 'A foundation for the study of group decision support systems', *Management Science*, 33 (5), 589-609.

Ellis *et al* (1991). 'Groupware. Some issues and experiences', *Communications of the ACM*, 34 (1): 39-58.

Ginsburg, M. and Duliba, K. (1997). 'Enterprise-Level Groupware Choices: Evaluating Lotus Notes and Intranet-Based Solutions', *Computer Supported Cooperative Work: The Journal of Collaborative Computing*, 6: 201–225.

Grudin, J. (1994a). 'CSCW: History and focus', *IEEE Computer*, 27 (5): 19-26.

Grudin, J., (1994b). Groupware and social dynamics: Eight challenges for developers. *Communications of the ACM*, 37 (1), 92-105.

Hills, M. (1997). *Intranet as GroupWare*, John Wiley and Sons, New York, NY.

ISWorld Net (1998) CVOC project information, Retrieved June 2003 from: <http://isds.bus.lsu.edu/cvoc/about/projects.html>.

Kay, H. (2001). 'A History Lesson', Computerworld, Retrieved June 2003 from: <http://www.computerworld.com/softwaretopics/software/groupware/story/0,10801,65574,00.html>.

Lotus Corporation, Groupware (white paper), 1996.

Lynch, K., Snyder, J., Vogel, D. (1990) 'The Arizona Analyst Information System: Supporting Collaborative Research on International Technology Trends', in Gibbs, S., Verrijn-Stuart, A. (Eds.) *Multiuser Interfaces and Applications*, North-Holland, pp. 159-174.
Malone, T., Lai, K., Fry, C., (1992), 'Experiments with OVAL: A Radically Tailorable Tool for Cooperative Work,' In *Proceedings CSCW 1992*, ACM.
O'Hara-Devereaux, M., and Johansen, R. (1994). *Globalwork*. San Francisco: Jossey-Bass
Rodden, T. (1991) 'A survey of CSCW systems', *Interacting with Computers*, vol. 3 (3): 319-353.
Siviter, D., Petre, M. and Klein, B. (1997). 'Harnessing Technology for effective Inter- and Intra-institutional Collaboration', Proceedings of the ACM-SIGCSE/SIGCUE conference on Integrating Technology into Computer Science Education, Uppsala, Sweden, June 1997, ACM ISBN 1-58113-012-0, pp. 70-93.
Sun Microsystems (2003). Retrieved June 2003 from: <http://java.sun.com/j2ee/1.4/docs/tutorial/doc/JMS3.html>.
Trusted Information System (1998). 'Application Gateways and Stateful Inspection: A Brief Note Comparing and Contrasting', Revised: 1/22/98, Retrieved June 2003 from: <http://www.spirit.com/CSI/Papers/apgw+spf.html>.
Van Vleck, T. (2001). 'The History of Electronic Mail,' Retrieved June 2003 from: <http://www.multicians.org/thvv/mail-history.html>.
Weatherall, A. and Nunamaker, J. (1996) *Introduction to Electronic Meetings*, Electronic Meeting Services Ltd., UK.

Chapter 3

Advisory Group on Computer Graphics (AGOCG) (1998). 'The Role of ATM Networks – The Metropolitan Area Networks', Retrieved June 2003 from: <http://www.agocg.ac.uk/reports/mmedia/casestdy/ucl/atm.htm>.
Ajuja, M.K. and Carlye K.M. (1998). 'Network Structure in Virtual Organizations', *Journal of Computer-Mediated Communications*, 3 (4), June 1998. Retrieved June 2003 from: <http://www.ascusc.org/jcmc/vol3/issue4/ahuja.html>.
American Productivity and Quality Center (APQC) (2001). 'Building and Sustaining Communities of Practice: Continuing Success in Knowledge Management', Retrieved June 2003 from: <http://www.apqc.org/portal/apqc/site/generic2?path=/site/training/courses/building_cops.jhtml>.
Choi, S.Y., Stahal, D. O. and Whinston, A.B. (1997). 'Commerce on the Internet: What's Holding It Up?', *Intergovernmental Solutions Newsletter*, Retrieved June 2003 from: <http://cism.bus.utexas.edu/works/articles/intergov.html>.
Church, C. (2001). 'Chambers to Comdex: The Future is 'Net Impact'', Press Release, Nov. 12, 2001, Retrieved June 2003 from: <http://newsroom.cisco.com/dlls/ts_111201.html>.
Cisco Systems Inc. (2001) 'E-Learning', Retrieved June 2003 from: <http://www.cisco.com/warp/public/732/abc/applications/elearning.shtml>.
Fairhurst, G. (2001). 'Communications Engineering syllabus', Retrieved June 2003 from: <http://www.erg.abdn.ac.uk/users/gorry/eg3561/>.
FDM Technologies (2002). 'What is a Wireless LAN?', Retrieved June 2003 from: <http://www.fdmtech.co.uk/What%20is%20wlan.htm>.
FindVPN (2003) 'The Advantages of a VPN', Retrieved June 2003 from: <http://findvpn.com/articles/benefits.cfm>.

Fukuyama, F. (2002). 'The Virtual Handshake: E-Commerce and the Challenge of Trust', Public Policy, George Mason University, Retrieved June 2003 from: <http://www.ml.com/woml/forum/ecommerce1.htm>.

Henschel, P. (2001). 'Understanding and Winning the Never-Ending Search for Talent: The Manager's Core Work in the NewEconomy', *LineZINE,* Fall 2001.

Indiana University (1996), 'Unix Workstation System Administration Education Certification Course', Retreived June 2003 from: <http://www.ussg.iu.edu/usail/network/nfs/network_layers.html>.

Intrinsix Network Projects Group, ISO Layers (2002). Retrieved June 2003 from: <http://www.intrinsix.com/Publications/ISOlayers.htm>.

Kaplan, S. and Bartlett, P. (2002). 'Creating Communities for Collaboration and Learning', Icohere White Paper, Retrieved June 2003 from: <http://www.icohere.com/Community_Collaboration_&_Learning.pdf>.

Loral (2000) 'Loral Cyberstar Press Release', June 23, 2000. Retrieved June 2003 from: <http://www.loral.com/inthenews/000623.html>.

Merriam-Webster (2003). *Webster's New World Dictionary and Thesaurus*, (pp. 119). USA: Macmillan. Also available at <http://www.m-w.com/cgi-bin/dictionary>.

Searchnetworking.com (2003). Definition of VPN, Retrieved June 2003 from: <http://searchnetworking.techtarget.com/sDefinition/0,,sid7_gci213324,00.html>.

Wave Systems (2003). 'Trusted Client: The Strategic New Building Block of the Digital Economy', Retrieved June 2003 from: <http://www.wavesys.com/technology/trust_client.html>.

Chapter 4

Applegate, L. (1995), *Managing in an Information Age: IT Challenges and Opportunities*, Boston: Harvard Business School Publishing, 9-196-004.

Bleeker, S.E. (1994), 'The virtual organization', *The Futurist*, (March-April), 9-14.

Carter, B.C. (1999). *Infinite Wealth: A New World Of Collaboration And Abundance In The Knowledge Era.* Butterworth Heinemann.

Chandler, A.D. (1977), *The Visible Hand*, Boston: Harvard University Press, 2, 10.

Chessbrough, H.W. and Teece, D. J. (1996). 'When is virtual virtuous? Organizing for innovation', *Harvard Business Review*; 74 (1), 65-73.

Clancy, T. (1994). 'The latest word from thoughtful executives', *Academy of Management Executive*, 8 (5), 8-10.

Connelly, J. (1995). 'Let's hear it for the office', *Fortune*, March 6, 1995; 221-222.

Davidow, W.H. and Malone, M. S. (1992). *The Virtual Corporation; New York: Harper Business,* 1, 19.

Deming, W. E. (1991). *Out of the Crisis,* Cambridge: MIT Press; pp. 24-25, 115-117.

Dess, G.G., Rasheed A. M., Mc Laughlin, K.J., and Priem, R. L. (1995). 'The new corporate architecture', *Academy of Management Executive*, 9 (3), 7-18.

Foster, I. and Kesselman, C. (1999). *The Grid, Blueprint for a Future Computing Infrastructure*. San Francisco, Morgan Kaufmann.

Gillmor, S. (2002). 'Grid Will Hunting', *InfoWorld*, Feb. 22, 2002 issue, Retrieved June 2003 from <http://www.infoworld.com/articles/op/xml/02/02/25/020225opcurve.xml>.

Gray, P. (1995). 'Understanding buzzwords', *Information Systems Management*, Spring; 80-83.

Handy, C.F. (1995); 'Trust and the virtual organization', *Harvard Business Review*, 73 (2), 65-71.

Herold, R. and Warigon, S. (1998). 'Extranet Audit and Security,' *Computer Security Journal*, Vol. XIV, No. 1, 35-44.

Kirk, Margaret O. (1996). 'The virtual office bumps into some very real limits', *New York Times* (Late New York Edition); March 3, Section 3; 10.

McConnell, M. (2002). 'Information Assurance in the Twenty-First Century', IEEE Special on Security and Privacy, Retrieved June 2003 from: <http://www.computer.org/security/supplement1/mcc/>.

Miller, H.E. and Engemann, K.J. (1997). 'The Role of Information Technology in Managing Virtual Organizations', Paper presented at the Fourth International Conference on Social Values; St. Catherine's College; University of Oxford, England; July 6-9, 1997. Retrieved June 2003 from: <http://www.muhlenberg.edu/depts/abe/business/miller/virorg.html>.

Miller, D.B., Clemens, E.K., and Row, M. C. (1993). 'Information technology and the global virtual corporation', in Bradley, S.P., ed., *Globalization, Technology, and Competition*, Boston: Harvard Business School Press, 282-308.

Munro, M. (2003). 'Creating the Agile Organization', Oblix Executive ViewPoint, Retrieved June 2003 from: <http://www.oblix.com/pointofentry/poe_ex_agileorganization.html>.

Rayport, J.F. and Sviokla, J.J. (1995). 'Exploiting the virtual value chain', *Harvard Business Review*, 73 (6), 75-85.

Senge, P. (1994). *The Fifth Discipline Fieldbook*. New York: Doubleday.

Schroeder, R. (1994). 'Cyberculture, cyborg Post-modernism and the sociology of virtual reality technologies', *Futures*, 26 (5), 519-528.

Upton, D. M. and McAfee, A. (1996). 'The real virtual factory', *Harvard Business Review*, 74 (4), 123-133.

Chapter 5

Allen, M.W. and Hayes, S.J. (2001). 'Raising the Stakes in the Staffing Game: Corporations Are Ready for Web-Enabled Procurement of Professional Services,' *SunTrust Robinson Humphrey Capital Markets, Business and Technology Services,* September 6, 2001, p. 3.

Canadian Marconi Company (1997). 'Visualization Technologies', Canadian Aircraft Design, Manufacturing and Repair & Overhaul Technology Road Map (Ontario Pilot Project) Critical Technology Reports.

Casado, E. (2002). 'Thinking Outside the Lines', *Intelligent Enterprise*, June 28, 2002, Retreived June 2003 from: <http://www.intelligententerprise.com/020628/511feat3_1.shtml>.

Clemons, E. K., Reddi, S. P. & Row, M. C. (1993). 'The Impact of Information Technology on the Organization of Economic Activity: "The Move to The Middle" Hypothesis,' *Journal of Management Information Systems,* 10 (2), Fall 1993, 9-35.

Fingar, P. (2000). 'Transforming the supply chain', *Logistics Management & Distribution Report*, 04/01/2000 Supplement, Available online at URL: <http://home1.gte.net/pfingar/logisticsmag04-00.htm>.

Forrester, J. W. (1961). *Industrial Dynamics*, M.I.T. Press, 1961

Information Week (1997). 'Manufacturing Systems Orders From Chaos,' *Information Week*, June 23, 1997.

Langhoff, J. (1997) 'Chain of Command: Forging New Partnerships, Building Bigger Profit Margins,' *Oracle Magazine*, Profit, November, 1997. Retreived June 2003 from: <http://www.oramag.com/profit/97-Nov/chain.html>.

Leymann, F. and D. Roller, D. (1997). 'Workflow-based Applications', *IBM Systems Journal*, 36(1), 1997.

NAPCP (2001) 'Corporate E-procurement Benchmark Survey Results', Palmer and Associates, Retrieved June 2003 from: <http://www.napcp.org/napcp/napcp.nsf/(ItemsByItemName)/EProcurementSurvey?OpenDocument>.

Pastore, M. (2001) 'The Future of E-Procurement? We'll Wait and See', Retreived June 2003 from: <http://cyberatlas.internet.com/markets/b2b/article/0,1323,10091_873291,00.html>.

Sawyer, C.A. (2001). 'Mach Speed Product Development: Inside the Skunk Works', *Automotive Design and Production*, Retrieved June 2003 from: <http://www.autofieldguide.com/articles/090107.html>.

Sieber, P and Griese, J. (eds) (1999). 'Organizational Virtualness and Electronic Commerce', Proc. 2nd Int'l VoNet Workshop, Zurich, Sept. 1999. <http://www.virtual-organization.net>.

Silvas, R.G., Baker, K. J., Wilcox, S. J. and Reuben, R. L. (2000). 'The Adaptability of a Tool Wear Monitoring System Under Changing Cutting Conditions', *Mechanical Systems and Signal Processing* 14(2), 287-298. Retreived June 2003 from: <http://www.idealibrary.com>.

Stough, S. Eom, S. and Buckenmyer, J. (2000) 'Virtual teaming: a strategy for moving your organization into the new millennium', *Industrial Management & Data Systems*, 100 (8), 370-378.

Szygenda, R. (1999). 'Information's Competitive Edge,' *Information Week*, February 8, 1999. Retreived June 2003 from: <http://www.informationweek.com/720/gmcorp.htm>.

INDEX